Verse Plays

THE MACMILLAN COMPANY
NEW YORK . BOSTON . CHICAGO . DALLAS
ATLANTA . SAN FRANCISCO

MACMILLAN & CO., Limited
LONDON . BOMBAY . CALCUTTA
MELBOURNE

THE MACMILLAN CO. OF CANADA, Ltd.
TORONTO

Verse Plays

By

John Masefield

New York
The Macmillan Company

1925

PRINTED IN THE UNITED STATES OF AMERICA
BY THE BERWICK AND SMITH COMPANY

INTRODUCTION

Sometimes the writers of prose ask: "Why do people write verse? Why do they write plays in verse?"

They add, that "since people in everyday life speak prose, it is easier to follow a play in which the actors speak prose." "Let these verse-writers," (they add) "be like their even Christian and write something that men can follow."

To every man his liking. Men write verse because they like thought of a certain quality and are touched by certain rhythms. They write plays in verse when they feel that their subjects demand it.

If playwrights were concerned solely with the characters and events of everyday life, they might find prose a sufficient instrument: but the playwright's art is not so limited: often a playwright is not concerned with the events of everyday life, but with dealings of the Gods, elements in the soul of man and the fables of a nation. He is then not writing of the accidents and incidents of personality, but of the heart of life as it is displayed at great moments. His theme then demands a language and a movement other than those of daily life: it becomes of the nature of religion and demands a ritual.

"Yet," (the writers of prose add), "nobody wants plays in verse: nobody goes to them."

That is not true. All over England, little companies of people are playing plays in verse because they enjoy them and prefer them. Great movements begin among little companies. Eighteen hundred years ago little companies of Christians looked at the majesty of the pagan world as a thing almost impossible even to attempt to overcome. In direct conflict, it would perhaps have been impossible to overcome, but by the patient endeavour of little companies for a thousand years the thing was done, and those companies raised themselves theatres where their rites could be fittingly performed.

JOHN MASEFIELD.

Oxford, 1925

CONTENTS

GOOD FRIDAY

A DRAMATIC POEM

GOOD FRIDAY

PERSONS

Pontius Pilate, Procurator of Judæa
Procula, His Wife.
Longinus, A Centurion.
A Jew, Leader of the Rabble.
A Madman.
A Sentry.
Joseph of Ramah.
Herod.
Soldiers, Servants, the Jewish Rabble, Loiterers, Idlers.

GOOD FRIDAY
A DRAMATIC POEM

THE SCENE

The Pavement, or Paved Court, outside the Roman Citadel in Jerusalem. At the back is the barrack wall, pierced in the center with a double bronze door, weathered to a green color. On the right and left sides of the stage are battlemented parapets overlooking the city. The stage or pavement is approached by stone steps from the front, and by narrow stone staircases in the wings, one on each side, well forward. These steps are to suggest that the citadel is high up above the town, and that the main barrack gate is below. THE CHIEF CITIZEN, THE RABBLE, JOSEPH, THE MADMAN, HEROD, *and* THE LOITERERS, *etc., enter by these steps.* PILATE, PROCULA, LONGINUS, THE SOLDIERS *and* SERVANTS *enter by the bronze doors.*

PILATE

Longinus.

LONGINUS

Lord.

PILATE

[*Giving scroll.*] Your warrant. Take the key.
Go to Barabbas' cell and set him free,
The mob has chosen him.

LONGINUS

And Jesus?

PILATE

Wait.

He can be scourged and put outside the gate,
With warning not to make more trouble here.
See that the sergeant be not too severe.
I want to spare him.

3

LONGINUS

And the Jew, the Priest,

Outside?

PILATE

I'll see him now.

LONGINUS

Passover Feast
Always brings trouble, Lord. All shall be done.
Dismiss?

PILATE

Dismiss. [*Exit* LONGINUS.]
　　　　　There's blood about the sun,
This earthquake weather presses on the brain.
　　　　　　　　[*Enter* PROCULA]
You?

PROCULA

Dear, forgive me, if I come again
About this Jesus, but I long to know
What Herod said. Did he dismiss him?

PILATE

　　　　　　　　　No.
He sent him back for me to try,
The charge being local.

PROCULA

Have you tried him?

PILATE

　　　　　　　　　　Ay,
Henceforth he will be kept outside the walls,
Now, listen, wife: whatever dream befalls,
Never again send word to me in Court
To interrupt a case. The Jews made sport
Of what you dreamed and what you bade me fear
About this Jesus man. The laws are clear.
I must apply them, asking nothing more

Than the proved truth.   Now tell me of your dream:
What was it?   Tell me then.

PROCULA

I saw a gleam
Reddening the world out of a blackened sky,
Then in the horror came a hurt thing's cry
Protesting to the death what no one heard.

PILATE

What did it say?

PROCULA

A cry, no spoken word
But crying, and a horror, and a sense
Of one poor man's naked intelligence,
Pitted against the world and being crushed.
Then, waking, there was noise; a rabble rushed
Following this Jesus here, crying for blood,
Like beasts half-reptile in a jungle mud.
And all the horror threatening in the dim,
In what I dreamed of, seemed to threaten him. . . .
So in my terror I sent word to you,
Begging you dearly to have nought to do
With that wise man.

PILATE

I grant he says wise things.
Too wise by half, and too much wisdom brings
Trouble, I find.   It disagrees with men.
We must protect him from his wisdom then.

PROCULA

What have you done to him?

PILATE

Made it more hard
For him to wrangle in the Temple yard
Henceforth, I hope.

[*Enter* LONGINUS]

PROCULA

You have not punished him?

PILATE

Warned him.

LONGINUS

The envoy from the Sanhedrim
Is here, my lord.

PILATE

Go. I must see him. Stay.
You and your women, keep within to-day.
It is the Jewish Feast and blood runs high
Against us Romans when the zealots cry
Songs of their old Deliverance through the land.
Stay, yet. Lord Herod says that he has planned
To visit us to-night, have all prepared.

PROCULA

I would have gone to Herod had I dared,
To plead for this man Jesus. All shall be
Made ready. Dear, my dream oppresses me. [*Exit.*]

PILATE

It is this earthquake weather: it will end
After a shock. Farewell.
[*Enter* CHIEF CITIZEN]

CHIEF CIT.

Hail, Lord and friend.
I come about a man in bonds with you,
One Jesus, leader of a perverse crew
That haunts the Temple.

PILATE

Yes, the man is here.

CHIEF CIT.

Charged with sedition?

PILATE

It did not appear
That he had been seditious. It was proved
That he had mocked at rites which people loved.
No more than that. I have just dealt with him.
You wish to see him?

CHIEF CIT.

No, the Sanhedrim
Send me to tell you of his proved intent.
You know how, not long since, a prophet went
Through all Judæa turning people's brains
With talk of One coming to loose their chains?

PILATE

John the Baptizer whom old Herod killed.

CHIEF CIT.

The Jews expect that word to be fulfilled,
They think that One will come. This Jesus claims
To be that Man, Son of the Name of Names,
The Anointed King who will arise and seize
Israel from Rome and you. Such claims as these
Might be held mad in other times than ours.

PILATE

He is not mad.

CHIEF CIT.

But when rebellion lowers
As now, from every hamlet, every farm,
One word so uttered does unreckoned harm.

PILATE

How do you know this?

CHIEF CIT.

From a man, his friend,
Frightened by thought of where such claims would end.
There had been rumors, yet we only heard
The fact but now.   We send you instant word.

PILATE

Yes.   This is serious news.   Would I had known.
But none the less, this Jesus is alone.
A common country preacher, as men say,
No more than that, he leads no big array:
No one believes his claim?

CHIEF CIT.

At present, no.
He had more friends a little while ago,
Before he made these claims of being King.

PILATE

You know about him then?

CHIEF CIT.

His ministering
Was known to us, of course.

PILATE

And disapproved?

CHIEF CIT.

Not wholly, no; some, truly; some we loved.
At first he only preached.   He preaches well.

PILATE

What of?

CHIEF CIT.

Of men, and of escape from hell
By good deeds done.   But when he learned his power
And flatterers came, then, in an evil hour,

As far as I can judge, his head was turned.
A few days past, from all that we have learned
He made this claim, and since persists therein.
Deluders are best checked when they begin.
So, when we heard it from this frightened friend,
We took this course to bring it to an end.

PILATE

Rightly. I thank you. Do I understand
That friends have fallen from him since he planned
To be this King?

CHIEF CIT.

They have, the most part.

PILATE

Why?

What makes them turn?

CHIEF CIT.

The claim is blasphemy
Punished by death under the Jewish laws.

PILATE

And under ours, if sufficient cause
Appear, and yet, if all the Jews despise
This claimant's folly, would it not be wise
To pay no heed, not make important one
Whom all contemn?

CHIEF CIT.

His evil is not done.
His claim persists, the rabble's mind will turn.
Better prevent him, Lord, by being stern.
The man has power.

PILATE

That is true, he has.

CHIEF CITIZEN

His is the first claim since the Baptist was,
Better not let it thrive.

PILATE

It does not thrive.

CHIEF CIT.

All ill weeds prosper, Lord, if left alive.
The soil is ripe for such a weed as this.
The Jews await a message such as his,
The Anointed Man, of whom our Holy Books
Prophesy much.   The Jewish people looks
For Him to come.

PILATE

These ancient prophecies
Are drugs to keep crude souls from being wise.
Time and again Rome proves herself your friend,
Then some mad writing brings it to an end.
Time and again, until my heart is sick.
Dead prophets spreading madness in the quick.
And now this Jesus whom I hoped to save.
Have you the depositions?

CHIEF CIT.

Yes, I have.

PILATE

Give me.

CHIEF CIT.

This is the docquet.

PILATE

This is grave.

CHIEF CIT.

I thought that you would think so.

PILATE

I will learn

What he can say to this and then return.
Wait. I must speak. Although I shall not spare
Anyone, man or woman, who may dare
To make a claim that threatens Roman rule,
I do not plan to be a priestly tool.
I know your Temple plots; pretend not here
That you, the priest, hold me, the Roman, dear.
You, like the other Jews, await this King
Who is to set you free, who is to ding
Rome down to death, as your priests' brains suppose.
This case of Jesus shows it, plainly shows.
He and his claim were not at once disowned;
You waited, while you thought "He shall be throned,
We will support him, if he wins the crowd."
You would have, too. He would have been endowed
With all your power to support his claim
Had he but pleased the rabble as at first.
But, since he will not back the priestly aim,
Nor stoop to lure the multitude, you thirst
To win my favor by denouncing him.
This rebel does not suit the Sanhedrim.
I know. . . . The next one may.

CHIEF CIT.

You wrong us, Sire.

PILATE

Unless he blench, you 'complish your desire
With Jesus, though; there is no king save Rome
Here, while I hold the reins. Wait till I come.

[*Exit* PILATE]

THE MADMAN

Only a penny, a penny,

Lilies brighter than any
White lilies picked for the Feast.

       [*He enters, tapping with his stick*]
I am a poor old man who cannot see,
Will the great noble present tell to me
If this is the Paved Court?

        CHIEF CIT.
         It is.

        MADMAN
            Where men
Beg for a prisoner's freedom?

        CHIEF CIT.
         Yes.   What then?

        MADMAN
I come to help the choosing.

        CHIEF CIT.
         You can go.

        MADMAN
Where, lord?

        CHIEF CIT.
Why, home.   You hear that noise below,
Or are you deaf?

        MADMAN
      No, lordship, only blind.

        CHIEF CIT.
Come this-day-next-year if you have the mind.
This year you come too late, go home again.

        MADMAN
Lord.   Is the prisoner loosed?

CHIEF CIT.
                    Yes, in the lane.
Can you not hear them cry "Barabbas" there?

MADMAN
Barabbas, Lord?

CHIEF CIT.
          The prisoner whom they bear
In triumph home.

MADMAN
          Barabbas?

CHIEF CIT.
                    Even he.

MADMAN
Are not you wrong, my Lord?

CHIEF CIT.
               Why should I be?

MADMAN
There was another man in bonds, most kind
To me, of old, who suffer, being blind.
Surely they called for him? One Jesus? No?

CHIEF CIT.
The choice was made a little while ago.
Barabbas is set free, the man you name
Is not to be released.

MADMAN
          And yet I came
Hoping to see him loosed.

CHIEF CIT.
               He waits within
Till the just pain is fitted to his sin.

It will go hard with him, or I mistake.
Pray God it may.

MADMAN

I sorrow for his sake.

CHIEF CIT.

God's scathe.

[*Enter more* JEWS]

MADMAN

A penny for the love of Heaven.
A given penny is a sin forgiven.
Only a penny, friends.

FIRST CIT.

The case was proved.   He uttered blasphemy.
Yet Pilate gives him stripes: the man should die.

THIRD CIT.

Wait here awhile.   It is not over yet.
This is the door, the man shall pay his debt.
After the beating they will let him go
And we shall catch him.

SECOND CIT.

We will treat him so

That he will not be eager to blaspheme
So glibly, soon.

THIRD CIT.

We will.

FIRST CIT.

Did Pilate seem

To you, to try to spare him?

SECOND CIT.

Ay, he did,

The Roman dog.

THIRD CIT.

We will not.

SECOND CIT.

God forbid.

FIRST CIT.

Well, we'll stay here.

SECOND CIT.

We will anoint this King.

CHIEF CIT.

You talk of Jesus?

FIRST CIT.

Yes.

CHIEF CIT.

I had to bring
News from the Temple but a minute past,
To-day is like to be King Jesus' last.

FIRST CIT.

So?

CHIEF CIT.

It is sure.   Wait here a little while.

FIRST CIT.

We mean to, Lord.   His tongue shall not defile
Our Lord again, by God.

CHIEF CIT.

By a happy chance
There came a hang-dog man with looks askance,
Troubled in mind, who wished to speak with us.
He said that he had heard the man speak thus
That he was the Messiah, God in man.
He had believed this, but his doubts began
When Jesus, not content, claimed further things;
To be a yoke upon the necks of Kings,

Emperor and Priest.   Then, though he found him kind
In friendship, he was troubled.   With bowed mind
He came to us and swore what Jesus claimed.
This Emperor over Kings will now be tamed.

VOICES

Will Pilate back the priests?

CHIEF CIT.

He cannot fail.
It threatens Roman power.

A VOICE

Listen, friends,
Pilate is coming; hark! the sitting ends.
No.   'Tis the Bench.

[*The bench is set by* SLAVES]

What will Lord Pilate do?

[THE SLAVES *do not answer*]

You Nubian eunuchs answer to the Jew.
Is the man cast?

A SLAVE

The circumcised will see
When Rome is ready.

[*Goes in and shuts the door*]

A VOICE

There.   They nail a tree.
They make a cross, for those are spikes being driven.
He's damned.

A VOICE

Not so, he still may be forgiven.
The cross may be for one of those two thieves.

A VOICE

I had forgotten them.

A Voice

This man believes
That Pilate was inclined to let him go.

Second Cit.

That was before this charge came.

A Voice
                              Even so
This Roman swine is fond of swine like these.

A Voice

Come, Pilate, come.

A Voice
                              He will not have much ease
This Paschal Feast, if Jesus is not cast.

A Voice

There is the door.   Lord Pilate comes at last.
No.   'Tis the trumpet.
                    [A Trumpeter *comes out*]

Voices
                    Blow the trumpet, friend.

A Voice

Roman.   Recruit.   When will the sitting end?

Voices

Fling something at him.   Roman.

A Voice
                              O, have done.
He will not hang until the midday sun.
And we shall lose our sleeps.   Let sentence pass.

A Voice

[*Singing.*]   As I came by the market I heard a woman sing:

"My love did truly promise to wed me with a ring,
But, oh, my love deceived me and left me here forlorn
With my spirit full of sorrow, and my baby to be born."

A Voice

Why are you standing here?

A Voice

  I came to see.

A Voice

O, did you so?

A Voice

  Why do you look at me?

A Voice

You were his friend: you come from Galilee.

A Voice

I do not.

A Voice

  Yes, you do.

A Voice

  I tell you, No.

A Voice

You know this man quite well.

A Voice

  I do not know

One thing about him.

A Voice

  Does he know the cur?

A Voice

Ay, but denies.   He was his follower.

A VOICE
I was not.

A VOICE
Why, I saw you in the hall,
I watched you.

A VOICE
I was never there at all.

A VOICE
So he would be a King.

A VOICE
That was the plan.

A VOICE
I swear to God I never saw the man.

A VOICE
He did; you liar; fling him down the stair.

A VOICE
I did not, friends.   I hate the man, I swear.

VOICES
You swear too much for truth, down with him, sons.
Leave him, here's Pilate.
    [*Enter* LONGINUS *and* SOLDIERS]

LONGINUS
Stand back.   Keep further back.   Get down the stair,
Stop all this wrangling.   Make less babble there.
Keep back yet further.   See you keep that line.
Silence.   These Jewish pigs.

THE JEWS
The Roman swine.

[Enter PILATE]

PILATE

Longinus.

LONGINUS

Lord.

PILATE

No Jew here thinks him King.
They want his blood.

LONGINUS

They would want anything
That would beguile the hours until the Feast.

PILATE

I would be glad to disappoint the priest.
I like this Jesus man.   A man so wise
Ought not to end through crazy prophecies.
Still, he persists.

LONGINUS

They are a stubborn breed.
The medicine Cross is what they mostly need.

PILATE

Still, this man is, in fact, a kind of king,
A God beside these beasts who spit and sting,
The best Jew I have known.

LONGINUS

He had his chance.

PILATE

O, yes, he had.   We'll let the Jews advance
Into the court.   I tried to set him free.
Still, if he will persist, the thing must be.
And yet I am sorry.

Longinus

I am sorry, too.
He seemed a good brave fellow, for a Jew.
Still, when a man is mad there is no cure
But death, like this.

Pilate

I fear so.

Longinus

I am sure.

Shall I begin?

Pilate

Yes.

Longinus

Sound the Assembly. [*Trumpet.*]

Sound

The Imperial call. [*Trumpet.*]

Pilate

You people, gathered round,
Behold your King.

Voices

Our King. I see him. Where?
That heap of clothes behind the soldiers there.
He has been soundly beaten. Look, he bleeds.
A cross on Old Skull Hill is what he needs.

Pilate

What would you, then, that I should do to him?

Voices

Stone the blasphemer, tear him limb from limb,
Kill him with stones, he uttered blasphemy,
Give him to us, for us to crucify.
Crucify!

PILATE

Would you crucify your King?

VOICES

He is no King of ours; we have no King
But Cæsar.   Crucify!

PILATE

Bring pen and ink.

LONGINUS

Hold up the prisoner, Lucius; give him drink.

PILATE

I come to sentence.

SERVANT

Writing things, my lord.

PILATE

Fasten the parchment to the piece of board.
So.   I will write.

VOICES

What does his writing mean?
It is the sentence of this Nazarene,
Condemning him to death.   A little while
And he'll be ours.   See Lord Pilate smile.
Why does he smile?

PILATE

Longinus.

LONGINUS

Lord.

PILATE

Come here.
Go to that man, that upland targeteer,
I want this writ in Hebrew.   Bid him write
Big easy letters that will catch the sight.

LONGINUS

I will, my lord.   Make way.
[*Exit* LONGINUS]

A VOICE

What's on the scroll?

A VOICE

It gives the prisoner into his control
To nail to death, the foul blaspheming beast.

A VOICE

D'you think he will be dead before the Feast?

A VOICE

They'll spear him if he lingers until dark.

A VOICE

When Feast begins he will be stiff and stark.
There's little life in him as it is.

VOICES

We'll hammer iron through those hands of his,
And through his feet, and when the cross is set
Jolt it; remember.   I will not forget.

A VOICE

Here comes the sentence.
[*Enter* LONGINUS]

A VOICE

Wait; it is not signed.

A VOICE

Come to the hill, you will be left behind.
I want a good place at the cross's foot.

A VOICE

I've got a stone for when they move the brute.

Besides, I mean to bait him on the way.
I'll spatter him with filth.

A Voice
No, come away.

Pilate
Imperial finding in the High Priest's suit.
In the name of Cæsar and of Rome. . . .

Longinus
                    Salute.

Pilate
I, Procurator of Judæa, say
That Jesus, called the King, be led away
To death by crucifixion, here and now.
In the name of Cæsar and of Rome. . . .

Longinus
                    We bow
To the sentence of the court.

Pilate
            See sentence done.
This is your warrant.

Longinus
Sentence shall be done.

Voices
Away, friends, hurry. Keep a place for me.
Get there before they come, then we shall see
All of the nailing and the fixing on.

Pilate
Longinus.

Longinus
    Lord.

PILATE

Display this scroll upon
The head of Jesus' cross, that men may read.
Wait; I'll declare it publicly.   Take heed. . . .
I add this word, that over Jesus' head
This scroll shall be displayed till he is dead.
Show it, Longinus.   Read it if you choose.

VOICES

"Jesus of Nazareth, the King of the Jews."
We'll make him King, we'll set him up in state.
At Golgotha.   Come; drag him through the gate.
Give him his cross.   Come, soldiers.

CHIEF CIT.

Israel, wait.
Wait.   I must speak.   Lord Pilate.

VOICES

Stand aside. . . .
Are we to miss his being crucified?

CHIEF CIT.

Wait.   Only wait.   One word.

MADMAN

Lord Pilate.   Lord.

SENTRY

Stand back.

MADMAN

I'll speak.

SENTRY

I'll tame you with the sword.

MADMAN

Lord Pilate, Jesus is an upright man,

I heard his teaching since it first began.
You are mistaken, Lord, you are misled.
Spare him, great King.

SENTRY

Get down.

MADMAN

Kill me instead.
He never said this thing. [*He is beaten aside*].

LONGINUS

The company,
Attention. Front. Take up the prisoner. By
The left, quick wheel. Down to the courtyard, wheel.

[THE TROOPS *go out by the doors, into the barracks, so as to reach the main gate from within. The* PRISONER *is not shown, but only suggested.*]

A VOICE

He cannot lift his cross, I saw him reel.

A VOICE

We'll find a man to bring it. Hurry, friends.
Three to be nailed.

A VOICE

The thieves will make good ends;
They always do. This fellow will die soon.

A VOICE

The troops will spear them all before full moon.
Come; watch them march them out.

Get mud to fling.

[*They hurry down the staircase* O. P. *side*]

CHIEF CIT.

[*To* PILATE.] Lord Pilate, do not write "Jesus the King,"
But that "He called himself, 'Jesus the King.'"

PILATE

Empty this water here. [SERVANT *does*]
Remove this board.
Take in the bench.

CHIEF CIT.

I have to ask, my lord,
That you will change the wording of your scroll,
My lord, it cuts my people to the soul.

PILATE

Tell Caius Scirrus that I want him. [*Exit* SERVANT.]
So. [*To* CHIEF CITIZEN.]
What I have written, I have written. Go.

[*Exit* CHIEF CITIZEN. PILATE *watches him. A yell below as the* TROOPS *march out from the main gate.* LONGINUS' *voice is heard shouting.*]

LONGINUS

Right wheel. Quick march.
Close up. Keep your files close.

[*A march is played, oboe and trumpet.* PILATE *goes in, the* TROOPS *salute, the bronze doors are closed, but a* SENTRY *stands outside them.* THE MADMAN *remains.*]

MADMAN

They cut my face, there's blood upon my brow.
So, let it run, I am an old man now,
An old, blind beggar picking filth for bread.
Once I wore silk, drank wine,
Spent gold on women, feasted, all was mine;
But this uneasy current in my head
Burst, one full moon, and cleansed me, then I saw
Truth like a perfect crystal, life its flaw,
I told the world, but I was mad, they said.

I had a valley farm above a brook,
My sheep bells there were sweet,
And in the summer heat
My mill wheels turned, yet all these things they took;
Ah, and I gave them, all things I forsook
But that green blade of wheat,
My own soul's courage, that they did not take.

I will go on, although my old heart ache.
Not long, not long.
Soon I shall pass behind
This changing veil to that which does not change,
My tired feet will range
In some green valley of eternal mind
Where Truth is daily like the water's song.

[*Enter the* CHIEF CITIZEN]

CHIEF CIT.

Where is Lord Pilate?

MADMAN
Gone within.

CHIEF CIT.
You heard
The way he spoke to me?

MADMAN
No, not a word.
The dogs so bayed for blood, I could not hear.
Ask the tall sentry yonder with the spear.

CHIEF CIT.
I wish to see Lord Pilate.

SENTRY
Stand aside.

CHIEF CIT.

Send word to him; I cannot be denied.
I have to see him; it concerns the State
Urgently, too, I tell you.

SENTRY

It can wait.

CHIEF CIT.

It may mean bloodshed.

SENTRY

Bloodshed is my trade.
A sentry's orders have to be obeyed
The same as God's that you were talking of.

CHIEF CIT.

I tell you, I must see him.

SENTRY

That's enough.

You cannot now.

MADMAN

The soldier's words are true.

CHIEF CIT.

Could you send word?

SENTRY

Sir, I have answered you.

CHIEF CIT.

Those words that Pilate wrote, the Hebrew screed,
May cause a riot.

MADMAN

Yes?

CHIEF CIT.

And death.

SENTRY

Indeed.
You got the poor man's life, what would you more?

CHIEF CIT.

Means to see Pilate.

SENTRY

As I said before,
You cannot. Stand away. A man like you
Ought to know better than to lead a crew
To yell for a man's blood. God stop my breath,
What does a man like you with blood and death?
Go to.

CHIEF CIT.

You will not send?

SENTRY

I will not send.

CHIEF CIT.

[*Going.*] You shall regret this.

SENTRY

Right. Goodbye, my friend.

CHIEF CIT.

Means will be found. [*Exit.*]

SENTRY

These priests, these preaching folk. [*Pause. Sings.*]
"Upon a summer morning, I bade my love goodbye,
In the old green glen so far away,
To go to be a soldier on biscuits made of rye."

It is darker than it was.

MADMAN

It is falling dark.

SENTRY

It feels like earthquake weather.   Listen.

MADMAN

Hark.

SENTRY

It sounded like a shock inside the walls.

MADMAN

God celebrates the madman's funerals.

SENTRY

The shouts came from the Temple.

MADMAN

Yes, they sing
Glory to God there, having killed their King.

SENTRY

You knew that man they are hanging?

MADMAN

Yes.   Did you?

SENTRY

Not till I saw him scourged.   Was he a Jew?

MADMAN

No.   Wisdom comes from God, and he was wise.
I have touched wisdom since they took my eyes.

SENTRY

So you were blinded?   Why?

MADMAN

Thinking aloud,
One Passover.

SENTRY

How so?

MADMAN

                 I told the crowd
That only a bloody God would care for blood.
The crowd kill kids and smear the lintel wood,
To honor God, who lives in the pure stars.

SENTRY

You must have suffered; they are angry scars.

MADMAN

There is no scar inside.

SENTRY

                 That may be so;
Still, it was mad; men do not wish to know
The truth about their customs, nor aught else.   [*Cries off.*]

MADMAN

They have nailed the teacher Jesus by those yells.

SENTRY

It is darker.   There'll be earthquake before night.
What sort of man was he?

MADMAN

               He knew the right
And followed her, a stony road, to this.

SENTRY

I find sufficient trouble in what is
Without my seeking what is right or wrong.

MADMAN

All have to seek her, and the search is long.

SENTRY

Maybe.

MADMAN

     And hard.

SENTRY

Maybe. [*Pause. Sings.*]
"I mean to be a captain before I do return,
Though the winters they may freeze and the summers they
    may burn,
I mean to be a captain and command a hundred men
And the women who. . ." [*A bugle call off.*]
There is recall.

[*The doors are opened and the* SENTRY *goes*]

MADMAN

The wild-duck, stringing through the sky,
Are south away.
Their green necks glitter as they fly,
The lake is gray,
So still, so lone, the fowler never heeds.
The wind goes rustle, rustle, through the reeds.

      *   *   *   *   *   *

There they find peace to have their own wild souls.
In that still lake,
Only the moonrise or the wind controls
The way they take,
Through the gray reeds, the cocking moorhen's lair,
Rippling the pool, or over leagues of air.

      *   *   *   *   *   *

Not thus, not thus are the wild souls of men.
No peace for those
Who step beyond the blindness of the pen
To where the skies unclose.
For them the spitting mob, the cross, the crown of thorns,
The bull gone mad, the saviour on his horns.

      *   *   *   *   *   *

Beauty and Peace have made
No peace, no still retreat,

No solace, none.
Only the unafraid
Before life's roaring street
Touch Beauty's feet,
Know Truth, do as God bade,
Become God's son.   [*Pause.*]

Darkness come down, cover a brave man's pain.
Let the bright soul go back to God again.
Cover that tortured flesh, it only serves
To hold that thing which other power nerves.
Darkness, come down, let it be midnight here,
In the dark night the untroubled soul sings clear. [*It darkens.*]

I have been scourged, blinded and crucified,
My blood burns on the stones of every street
In every town; wherever people meet
I have been hounded down, in anguish died. [*It darkens.*,]
The creaking door of flesh rolls slowly back.
Nerve by red nerve the links of living crack,
Loosing the soul to tread another track.

Beyond the pain, beyond the broken clay,
A glimmering country lies
Where life is being wise,
All of the beauty seen by truthful eyes
Are lilies there, growing beside the way.
Those golden ones will loose the torted hands,
Smooth the scarred brow, gather the breaking soul,
Whose earthly moments drop like falling sands
To leave the spirit whole.
Now darkness is upon the face of the earth. [*He goes.*]

  [PILATE *entering, as the darkness reddens to a glare*]

PILATE

This monstrous day is in the pangs of birth.

There was a shock.   I wish the troops were back
From Golgotha.   The heavens are more black
Than in the great shock in my first year's rule.
Please God these zealot pilgrims will keep cool
Nor think this done by God for any cause.
The lightning jags the heaven in bloody scraws
Like chronicles of judgment.   Now it breaks.
Now rain.

PROCULA

[*Entering.*]   O Pilate.

PILATE

What?

PROCULA

> For all our sakes
Speak.   Where is Jesus?

PILATE

He is crucified.

PROCULA

Crucified?

PILATE

Put to death.   My wife, I tried
To save him, but such men cannot be saved.
Truth to himself till death was all he craved.
He has his will.

PROCULA

So what they said is true.
O God, my God.   But when I spoke to you
You said that you had warned him.

PILATE

> That is so.
Another charge was brought some hours ago,
That he was claiming to be that great King
Foretold by prophets, who shall free the Jews.

This he persisted in.   I could not choose
But end a zealot claiming such a thing.

PROCULA

He was no zealot.

PILATE

Yes, on this one point.
Had he recanted, well.   But he was firm.
So he was cast.

PROCULA

The gouts of gore anoint
That temple to the service of the worm.
It is a desecration of our power.
A rude poor man who pitted his pure sense
Against what holds the world its little hour,
Blind force and fraud, priests' mummery and pretence,
Could you not see that this is what he did?

PILATE

Most clearly, wife.   But Roman laws forbid
That I should weigh, like God, the worth of souls.
I act for Rome, and Rome is better rid
Of these rare spirits whom no law controls.
He broke a statute, knowing from the first
Whither his act would lead, he was not blind.

PROCULA

No, friend, he followed hungry and athirst
The lonely exaltation of his mind.
So Rome, our mother, profits by his death,
You think so?

PILATE

Ay.

PROCULA

We draw securer breath,
We Romans, from his gasping on the cross?

PILATE

Some few will be the calmer for his loss.
Many, perhaps; he made a dangerous claim.
Even had I spared it would have been the same
A year, or two, from now.   Forget him, friend.

PROCULA

I have no part nor parcel in his end.
Rather than have it thought I buy my ease,
My body's safety, honor, dignities,
Life and the rest at such a price of pain
There [*she stabs her arm with her dagger*] is my blood, to wash
away the stain.
There.   There once more.   It fetched too dear a price.
O God, receive that soul in paradise.

PILATE

What have you done?

PROCULA

No matter; it atones.
His blood will clamor from the city stones.

PILATE

Go in.   No, let me bind it.

PROCULA

Someone comes.
A councillor, I think.   Ask what he wants.

[*Enter* JOSEPH]

JOSEPH

Greetings, Lord Pilate.

PILATE

And to you.

Joseph

[*To* Procula.]   And you.
[*To* Pilate.]   I have a boon to ask.

Procula

                    What can we do?

Joseph

Lord Pilate, may I speak?

Pilate

[*To* Procula.]   Go in.   [*She goes in.*]   Go on [*to* Joseph].

Joseph

The man called Christ, the follower of John,
Was crucified to-day by your decree.
[Pilate *bows.*]   He was my master, very dear to me.
I will not speak of that.   I only crave
Leave to prepare his body for the grave,
And then to bury him.   May I have leave?

Pilate

Yes, you may have him when the guards give leave.
Wait.   In a case like this, men may believe
That the dead master is not really dead.
This preaching man, this King, has been the head
Of men who may be good and mean no harm,
Whose tenets, none the less, have caused alarm
First to the priests, and through the priests to me.
I wish this preacher's followers to see
That teaching of this kind is to be curbed.
I mean, established truths may be disturbed,
But not the Jews, nor Rome.   You understand?

Joseph

I follow; yes.

PILATE

A riot might be fanned,
Such things have been, over the martyr's grave.

JOSEPH

His broken corpse is all his followers crave.

PILATE

Why, very well then.

JOSEPH

Will you give your seal?

PILATE

My seal? What for?

JOSEPH

That I may show the guard
And have the body.

PILATE

Gladly; but I feel . . .
Not yet; not until dark.

JOSEPH

It will be hard
To bury him to-night. . . the feast begins.

PILATE

I know, but still, when men are crucified . . .

JOSEPH

There is no hope of that. The man has died.

PILATE

Died? Dead already?

JOSEPH

Yes.

PILATE

'Tis passing soon.

JOSEPH

God broke that bright soul's body as a boon.
He died at the ninth hour.

PILATE

Are you sure?

JOSEPH

I saw him, Lord.

PILATE

I thought he would endure
Longer than that; he had a constant mind.

JOSEPH

The great soul burns the body to a rind.

PILATE

But dead, already; strange; strange.   [*Calling.*]
You in the court,
Send me Longinus here with his report.

A VOICE

I will, my lord.

PILATE

This teacher was your friend?

JOSEPH

Was, is, and will be, till the great world end;
Which God grant may be soon.

PILATE

I disagree
With teachers of new truth.   For men like me
There is but one religion, which is Rome.
No easy one to practise, far from home.
You come from Ramah?

JOSEPH

Yes.

PILATE

What chance is there

Of olives being good?

JOSEPH

They should be fair.

PILATE

You will not use Italian presses? No?

JOSEPH

Man likes his own, my lord, however slow;
What the land made, we say, it ought to use.

PILATE

Your presses waste; oil is too good to lose.
But I shall not persuade.

SERVANT

Longinus, lord.

PILATE

Make your report, centurion. Where's your sword?
What makes you come thus jangled? Are you ill?

LONGINUS

There was a shock of earthquake up the hill.
I have been shaken. I had meant to come
Before; but I was whirled . . . was stricken dumb.
I left my sword within. . . .

PILATE

Leave it. Attend.

Is the man, Jesus, dead? This is his friend
Who wants to bury him, he says he is.

LONGINUS

Jesus is out of all his miseries.
Yes, he is dead, my lord.

PILATE

Already?

LONGINUS

Yes.
The men who suffer most endure the less.
He died without our help.

JOSEPH

Then may I have
His body, Lord, to lay it in the grave?

PILATE

A sentry's there?

LONGINUS

Yes, Lord.

PILATE

Have you a scroll?
[*Takes paper.*] Right. Now some wax. [*Writes.*]
Give into his control
The body of the teacher; see it laid
Inside the tomb and see the doorway made
Secure with stones and sealed, then bring me word.
This privilege of burial is conferred
On the conditions I have named to you.
See you observe them strictly.

JOSEPH

I will do
All that himself would ask to show my sense
Of this last kindness. I shall go from hence
Soon, perhaps far; I give you thanks, my lord.
Now the last joy the niggard fates afford;
One little service more, and then an end
Of that divineness touched at through our friend. [*Exit.*]

PILATE

See that the tomb is sealed by dark to-night.
Where were you hurt, Longinus?   You are white.
What happened at the cross?

LONGINUS
                              We nailed him there
Aloft, between the thieves, in the bright air.
The rabble and the readers mocked with oaths,
The hangman's squad were dicing for his clothes.
The two thieves jeered at him.   Then it grew dark,
Till the noon sun was dwindled to a spark,
And one by one the mocking mouths fell still.
We were alone on the accursed hill
And we were still, not even the dice clicked,
Only the heavy blood-gouts dropped and ticked
On to the stone; the hill is all bald stone.
And now and then the hangers gave a groan.
Up in the dark, three shapes with arms outspread.
The blood-drops spat to show how slow they bled.
They rose up black against the ghastly sky,
God, Lord, it is a slow way to make die
A man, a strong man, who can beget men.
Then there would come another groan, and then
One of those thieves (tough cameleers those two)
Would curse the teacher from lips bitten through
And the other bid him let the teacher be.
I have stood much, but this thing daunted me,
The dark, the livid light, and long long groans
One on another, coming from their bones.
And it got darker and a glare began
Like the sky burning up above the man.
The hangman's squad stood easy on their spears
And the air moaned, and women were in tears,
While still between his groans the robber cursed.

The sky was grim: it seemed about to burst.
Hours had passed: they seemed like awful days.
Then . . . what was that?

PILATE

What? Where?

LONGINUS

A kind of blaze,

Fire descending.

PILATE

No.

LONGINUS

I saw it.

PILATE

Yes?

What was it that you saw?

LONGINUS

A fiery tress
Making red letters all across the heaven.
Lord Pilate, pray to God we be forgiven.

PILATE

"The sky was grim," you said, there at the cross.
What happened next?

LONGINUS

The towers bent like moss
Under the fiery figures from the sky.
Horses were in the air, there came a cry.
Jesus was calling God: it struck us dumb.
One said "He is calling God. Wait. Will God come?
Wait." And we listened in the glare. O sir,
He was God's son, that man, that minister,
For as he called, fire tore the sky in two,

The sick earth shook and tossed the cross askew,
The earthquake ran like thunder, the earth's bones
Broke, the graves opened, there were falling stones.

PILATE

I felt the shock even here.   So?

LONGINUS
Jesus cried
Once more and drooped, I saw that he had died.
Lord, in the earthquake God had come for him.
The thought of 't shakes me sick, my eyes are dim.

PILATE

Tell Scirrus to relieve you.

LONGINUS

Lord. . . .

PILATE
Dismiss.

Lie down and try to sleep; forget all this.
Tell Scirrus I command it.   Rest to-night.
Go in, Longinus, go.

LONGINUS

Thank you, Lord Pilate.

[*Exit* LONGINUS]

PILATE

[*Alone.*]   No man can stand an earthquake.   Men can bear
Tumults of water and of fire and air,
But not of earth, man's grave and standing ground;
When that begins to heave the will goes round.
Longinus, too.   [*Noise below.*]   Listen.
Does Herod come?

I heard his fifes.

[*The doors open.*   SERVANTS *enter*]

SERVANT

 Lord Herod is at hand;
Will it please your Lordship robe?

PILATE

       Sprinkle fresh sand,
For blood was shed to-day, here, under foot. [*He robes.*]
Well, that; the other clasp. [*Music off.*]

A VOICE

  Cohort. Salute.

PILATE

Leave torches at the door. Dismiss. [SERVANTS *go.*]
        He comes
Welcomed by everyone; the city hums
With joy when Herod passes. Ah, not thus
Do I go through the town. They welcome us
With looks of hate, with mutterings, curses, stones.

[*Enter* PROCULA]

Come, stand with me. Welcome Lord Herod here.
Welcome must make amends for barrack cheer.

[THE NUBIANS *hold torches at the door*]

[HEROD *enters*]

Come in, good welcome, Herod.

PROCULA

    Welcome, sir.

HEROD

To Rome, to Pilate, and to Beauty, greeting;
Give me your hands. What joy is in this meeting.
Pilate, again. You, you have hurt your hand?

PILATE

It is nothing, sir.

HEROD

Beauty has touched this hand,
A wound has followed.

PROCULA

What you please to call
Beauty, my lord, did nothing of the kind.
An earthen vessel tilted with a wall.

HEROD

May it soon mend. Now let me speak my mind.
Pilate, since you have ruled here, there have been
Moments of . . . discord, shall we say? between
Your government and mine. I am afraid
That I, the native here, have seldom made
Efforts for friendship with you.

PILATE

Come.

HEROD

I should
Have done more than I have, done all I could,
Healed the raw wound between the land and Rome,
Helped you to make this hellish town a home,
Not left it, as I fear it has been, hell
To you and yours cooped in a citadel
Above rebellion brewing. For the past
I offer deep regret, grief that will last,
And shame; your generous mind leaves me ashamed.

PILATE

Really, my lord.

PROCULA

These things must not be named.

PILATE

It is generous of you to speak like this,
But, Herod, hark.

PROCULA

If things have been amiss,

The fault was ours.

HEROD

No, the fault was mine.

Your generous act this morning was a sign
Of scrupulous justice done to me by you
For all these years, unnoticed hitherto,
Unrecognized, unthanked. I thank you now.
Give me your hand . . . so . . . thus.

PILATE

Herod, I bow

To what you say. To think that I have done
Something (I know not what) that has begun
A kindlier bond between us, touches home.
I have long grieved lest I have injured Rome
By failing towards yourself, where other men
Might have been wiser. . . . That is over, then?
Our differences henceforth may be discussed
In friendly talk together;

HEROD

So I trust.

PILATE

Give me your hand; I have long hoped for this.
I need your help, and you, perhaps, need mine.
The tribes are restless on the border-line,
The whole land seethes: the news from Rome is bad.
But this atones.

PROCULA

O, fully.

HEROD

I am glad.

PILATE

Let us go in.

HEROD

You lead.

PROCULA

A moment, one. . . .
You named a generous act that he had done. . . . ?

HEROD

This morning, yes; you sent that man to me
Because his crime was laid in Galilee.
A little thing, but still it touched me close;
It made me think how our disputes arose
When thieves out of your province brought to me
Were punished with a fine, perhaps set free,
Not sent to you to judge, as you sent him.
In future you will find me more a friend.
Or so I hope.

PILATE

Thanks.   May the gods so send
That this may lead to happier days for us.

VOICES OF THE CROWD

[*Who are now flocking in, among them* THE MADMAN.]   Herod
the good, Herod the glorious.
Long life to Herod.

PILATE

Come, the crowd begin. . . .

VOICES

Herod for ever.

PILATE

Let us go within. . . .

HEROD

Yes. By the by, what happened to the man?

I sent him back to you; a rumor ran
That he was crucified.

PILATE

He was.

HEROD

                    The priests
Rage upon points of doctrine at the feasts.

VOICES

God bless you, Herod; give you length of days, Herod.

HEROD

[*To the* CROWD].　Go home.　To God alone give praise.
This is Deliverance Night; go home, for soon
Over the dusty hill will come the moon,
And you must feast, with prayer to the Adored.
[*To* PILATE.]　He well deserved his death.

VOICES

                    God bless you, Lord.

PILATE

I'll lead the way. . . .

VOICES

Herod.

HEROD

[*To* PROCULA.]　 Lady, your hand.

PROCULA

There is a just man's blood upon the sand.
Mind how you tread.

[*They go in.　The bronze doors are closed.　The* CROWD *remains
for an instant watching the doors.*]

A VOICE

Herod the Fox makes friends with Pilate.　Why?

A Voice

He needs a Roman loan.

A Voice

Look at the sky,
The Paschal moon has risen.

A Voice

God is great.
Why did I linger here? I shall be late. [*Going.*]

A Voice

Good night and blessing.

A Voice

[*Going.*]   Pilate's color changed
When we cheered Herod.

A Voice

They have been estranged
A long while now; but now they will be friends. [*Going.*]

A Voice

What joy it is when Preparation ends.
Now to our Feast. Do you go down the stair?

A Voice

Yes, past the pools; will you come with me there?

A Voice

I love to walk by moonlight; let us go. [*They go.*]

A Voice

[*Singing.*] Friends, out of Egypt, long ago,
Our wandering fathers came,
Treading the paths that God did show

By pointing cloud and flame.
By land and sea His darkness and His light
Led us into His peace. . . . [*The voice dies away.*]

A VOICE

[*Off.*]   Good night.

[*Only* THE MADMAN *remains. He takes lilies from a box and
    begins to tie them in bunches.*]

MADMAN

Only a penny, a penny,
Lilies brighter than any,
Lilies whiter than snow.   [*He feels that he is alone.*]
Beautiful lilies grow
Wherever the truth so sweet
Has trodden with bloody feet,
Has stood with a bloody brow.
Friend, it is over now,
The passion, the sweat, the pains,
Only the truth remains.   [*He lays lilies down.*]

        *   *   *   *   *   *

I cannot see what others see;
Wisdom alone is kind to me,
Wisdom that comes from Agony.

        *   *   *   *   *   *

Wisdom that lives in the pure skies,
The untouched star, the spirit's eyes;
O Beauty, touch me, make me wise.

CURTAIN

PHILIP THE KING

A PLAY IN ONE ACT

PHILIP THE KING

PERSONS

Philip the Second of Spain
His Daughter, the Infanta
An English Prisoner
A Spanish Captain
Guards

SPIRITS

Indians
Don John of Austria
Escovedo
Don Alvaro de Bazan, the Marquis of Santa Cruz
Alonso de Leyva

TIME

At dawn in late September, 1588

SCENE

A little dark cell in Philip's palace

PHILIP THE KING

PHILIP

[*Kneeling*] Lord, I am that Philip whom Thou hast made King of half the world. Thou knowest, Lord, how great a fleet I have fitted out to destroy the English, who work evil against Thee. Lord, I beseech Thee, keep that great Armada now, as I trust, in battle on the English coast. Protect my ships, O Lord, from fire and pestilence, from tempest and shipwreck, and in the day of battle. Amen. Amen.

Lord, now that the battle is joined, grant us Thy victory, I beseech Thee. Amen. Amen.

Lord, I beseech Thee to have in Thy special keeping my beloved friend, Alonso de Leyva, now at sea with my fleet. Guard his ways, O Lord, that so he may come safely home to me. Amen. Amen.

Lord, of Thy mercy, I beseech Thee to send to me, if it be Thy will, some word or message from my fleet, that I may know Thy will concerning it, that my weary heart may find peace. Amen. Amen. [*He rises.*]

[*Enter the* PRINCESS]

PRINCESS

Has no news come?

PHILIP

None yet.

PRINCESS

Still nothing?

PHILIP

No.

PRINCESS

Two months now since they sailed and still no word.

PHILIP

The wind is foul; they cannot send.

PRINCESS

I know.

And yet what tales, what rumours we have heard.
How the heart sickens for the want of news.
Is that a courier?

PHILIP

No.

PRINCESS

What if we lose?

PHILIP

Why should we lose?

PRINCESS

Because of too much pride
Planning for glory not as scripture bade.

PHILIP

I am not proud nor hopeful, nor afraid.
But you are trembling, sweet, and heavy-eyed.

PRINCESS

I am afraid, for all night long
The spirit of Spain's committed wrong,
Nourished wherever a life was shed,
    Stood near my bed;
And all night long it talked to me
Of a trouble there is beyond the sea.
A trouble of war . . . I heard a horn
    Blowing forlorn,
And I knew that it came from far away,
From men of Spain in a pass at bay
Blowing for help; the beaten call
    None heeds at all.

And now I fear that we have angered Him
    Who makes pride dim.

PHILIP

What we have done with our might
Cannot be hateful to God.
He speaks with dreams in the night
That the tired heart turn home
And an end of brooding come.
My heart has flushed in His praise,
The glow in my heart took sail
In a fleet that darkens the sprays;
Sacrifice may not avail,
But the uttermost gift is wise.

PRINCESS

Yes, I believe that; and the deed is grand—
It is a mighty blow to deal for God.
But in my ear there rings
Ill-omened words about the pride of kings—
"Pride is the evil that destroys a land."

PHILIP

Brooding and watching waste you, you must sleep;
The hand of God will bring us through the deep.

PRINCESS

Amen, my father, but my heart is breaking.

PHILIP

You are too young for heart-break; let it be.

PRINCESS

There was another fear which kept me waking:
Spain's unborn monarchs came by night to me,
Each holding fewer of the Spanish gems
Here and abroad, each weaker in the soul.

With wearier brows and dimmer diadems,
And feebler fingers giving up control,
Till, as it seemed, a hundred years from now,
An idiot child was all the might of Spain,
And English spirits beat them on the brow,
Robbing their gems and binding them with chain.
And Spain's proud flag was draggled in the sea.
And then these shapes lamented, threatening me;
Saying that we began Spain's downfall here—
So grimly, father, that I shook with fear.

PHILIP

Child, these are only dreams.   I have learned this
Since I have been a king, that our concern
Is not with Hope nor Fear, but with what is,
Which, when we follow dreams, we cannot learn.
Be patient, child; besides, the wind has changed;
God's will must never find our hearts estranged:
The wind is north, the news may come to-day.
Ship after ship is running down the Bay
With news; God grant that it be happy news.

PRINCESS

Rest till it comes, dear father.

PHILIP

                    You can choose,
You who are young, whether to rest or no;
When one is old one sees the hours go.
Dear, they go fast from withered men like me.
You were my little daughter on my knee
When first this war with England was conceived.
Now you are this . . ., it would not be believed,
And nothing done, and still time hurrying by.
We are two grey old partners—Time and I:
Look at the work we do . . . you talk of rest.

PRINCESS

You call your Captains in and choose the best,
And make him do the work.

PHILIP

     Ah, you're a Queen,
That is what you would do, but I am King.
Kings have no beauty to make duty keen;
They have to supervise with whip and sting.

PRINCESS

You do not whip men; you are good and mild.

PHILIP

Artists and Kings do what they can, my child,
Not what they would.   It is not easy, dear,
Working with men, for men are only clay,
They crumble in the hand, or they betray
And time goes by, but no results appear—
Your little hands have happier work than mine.
Ah, little daughter, childhood is divine.

PRINCESS

I am no child now that the fleet has sailed;
I was till then, but now I realize
What it would cost my father if it failed.

PHILIP

Yes, it has cost some life, this enterprise.

PRINCESS

But all you had to do was give the word.

PHILIP

Ah, darling, many thousand men have heard
Orders from me since this attempt began
Seventeen years ago.   Full many a man

Who helped the earliest outlines of the plot
Died at his unknown task suspecting not
What pattern his life's colour helped to weave.
Child, if I told you, you would not believe
How this idea has triumphed on unchanged
Past great commanders' deaths, past faith estranged,
Past tyranny and bloodshed and ill-hap,
Treachery striking like a thunder-clap,
Murder, betrayal, lying, past all these,
Past the grim days when feelings had to freeze
Lest the great King should drop his mask of lies
And hint his purpose to the thwarted spies,
Past half a world of men and years of thought,
Past human hope, to be the thing I sought.
Now that the dice are scattered for the stakes,
I half forget that old affront of Drake's,
By which this war with England was begun.
O child, the labour that must first be done
Before a King can act!—unending work.
All the long days of beating down the Turk,
Then when Don John had thrust the Crescent down
(You cannot know) he plotted for the crown;
Don John, my Admiral, plotted against me.
He would have sunk the English in the sea,
But since he plotted, that was ended too.
Then a great world of labour still to do,
The French to check, and then the Portuguese,
Clearing myself a pathway through the seas.
Then, when my way was clear, my Admiral died,
The Marquis Santa Cruz, the unconquered guide,
The greatest sea commander of known times.
Seventeen years of subtleties and crimes.

But it is done. I have resolved those years,
Those men, those crimes, those great attempts, those tears,

Sorrows and terrors of a twisted earth,
Into this fleet, this death, this Dragon's birth;
I who have never seen it, nor shall see.

PRINCESS

I shall thank God that it was shown to me;
I saw it sail.

PHILIP

You saw my heart's blood, child.

PRINCESS

All a long summer day those ships defiled.
I never saw so many nor so grand;
They wandered down the tide and cleared the land,
And ranked themselves like pikemen, clump to clump.
Then in the silence came the Admiral's trump,
And from those hundreds of expectant ships,
From bells and cannonade and sailors' lips,
And from the drums and trumpets of the foot
Burst such a roaring thunder of salute
As filled my heart with wonder like a cup.
They cheered St. James's banner going up—
Golden St. James, whose figure blew out fair,
High on the flagship's mast in the blue air,
Rippling the gold.   Then all the city bells,
Fired like the singing spheres some spirit impels,
Rang in the rocking belfries, the guns roared,
Each human soul there shook like tautened cord.
And to that Christian march the singing priests
Bore up the blessed banners.   Even the beasts
Ramped at the challenge of that shouting crowd.
Then, as the wind came fair, the Armada bowed.
Those hundreds of great vessels, ranked in line,
Buried their bows and heaped the bubbled brine
In gleams before them.   So they marched; the van,
Led by De Leyva, like slipped greyhounds, ran

To spy the English. On the right and left
By Valdes and his friend the seas were cleft;
Moncada's gallies weltered like a weir,
Flanking Recalde, bringing up the rear,
While in the midst St. James's banner marched,
Blowing towards England till the flagpole arched.
Onward they swept the sea, the flagship's side
Smoked from her cannon's hail; she took her stride,
Leaned and stretched forward.

                     I was conscious then
That I beheld the greatest fleet that men
Ever sent seaward; all the world was there,
All nations that begem the crown you wear,
Pikemen of Rome, whose settled pikes had stood
Stern in full many a welter of man's blood.
Cunning Levantines, armed with crooked swords,
Venetians bronzed, the ocean's overlords,
Pisans and knights of Malta, Ferrarese,
Passionate half-bloods from the Indian seas,
Hollanders, Austrians, even English, come
To bring again religion to their home;
Spain too, our Andalusians, and the hale
Iberian Basquers used to hunt the whale—
The flower of the knighthood of the world
Mustered beneath the banner you unfurled.

       *   *   *   *   *   *

And that was but the half, for there in France
Was Parma's army ready to advance,
Death-coupled bloodhounds straining to the slip,
Waiting your navy's coming to take ship.
Father, such power awed me.

PHILIP

                     Time and I
Worked for long years.

PRINCESS

And when it had passed by
The bells were silent, and a sigh arose
Of joy in that fleet's pride, and grief for those
Who, even if all went well, had looked their last
On men and women who had made their past.
Then darkness came, and all that I could see
Was the horizon where the fleet must be—
A dimming skyline with a setting star.
It was as though they died; and now, who knows
What has befallen them, or where they are?
And night by sleepless night my trouble grows.
This daily silence has been hard to bear,
But now I dread news worse.

PHILIP

We must prepare,
Hoping the best, but ready for the worst;
But patient still, for rumour must come first—
Rumour and broken news and seamen's lies;
Patience, expecting nothing, is most wise.
If God vouchsafes it, we shall hear to-day.
Lighten your heart, my daughter.

PRINCESS

I will pray—
Pray for a Spanish triumph.

PHILIP

Pray for me.
Pray for God's cause adventured on the sea.

PRINCESS

I will; God help my prayer.

PHILIP

God help us both.   [*She goes.*]

Lord, I have laboured long to keep my oath,
And since my loved one died it has been hard.
O Lord, my God, in blessed mercy guard
My only friend De Leyva, now at sea;
Keep him, O Lord, and bring him home to me.
O Lord, be thou his bulwark and his guide;
I am so lonely since my loved one died.

How splendidly the nations hold their way,
Marching with banners through the fields of Time!
Who sees the withered King weary and grey,
Prompting it all with secret lust or crime?
Who guesses at the heavy brain behind?
I am Earth's greatest man; the world is blind.

[*He droops over his papers. Starting up*]

I have still strength, and I must read these scrolls,
Or else all goes to ruin; I must read.   [*He sleeps.*]

VOICES

Philip!

PHILIP

Who calls?

[*The* INDIANS *enter*]

VOICES

We are the Indian souls,
Loosed from the gold-mines where our brothers bleed.
We swell the tale of blood: we dug you gold;
We bore your burdens till we died of thirst;
We sweated in the mines or shook with cold,
Washing the gravel which the blast had burst.
We dived for pearls until our eyeballs bled;
You burned us till we told where treasure lay.

We were your Indian slaves, but we are dead;
Our red account is cast and you must pay.

A Voice

Our lives paid for your fleet; you pay for us.
The unjustly killed restore the balance thus.

A Voice

They flung my little baby to the hounds.

A Voice

They took my daughter from me for their lust.

A Voice

Even the weak are strong beyond life's bounds;
We myriad weak add power to the thrust.

Voices

Philip! Philip! Philip!
We gather from over the sea
To the justice that has to be
While the blind red bull goes on.
Philip! Philip! Philip!
We who are ciphers slain
In a tale of the pride of Spain
Are a part of her glory gone.

A Voice

We see them where our will can help their foes.

A Voice

Quick, brother, quick! another galleon goes!
Waken those sleeping gunners by the fire,
Or she'll escape unracked. [*They fade away.*]

Philip

The voices tire.

They go. I dreamed. I slept. My heavy head
Is drowsed. What man is that?

[DON JOHN *appears, with* ESCOVEDO *behind him*]

VOICE OF DON JOHN OF AUSTRIA

I am the dead;
I am your brother, Philip—brother John.

PHILIP

You corpse-fetch from the unclean grave, begone!
I had no brother.

DON JOHN

Would you never had!

PHILIP

You were a landmark of my father's sin,
Never my brother.

DON JOHN

I was that bright lad,
Your father's son, my brother; I helped win
Great glory for you, Philip.

PHILIP

I agreed
To overlook your bastardy, my friend,
So long as your bright talents served my need;
But you presumed, and so it had to end.

DON JOHN

My talents served you well.

PHILIP

They did, at first.

DON JOHN

I won the Battle of Lepanto for you.

PHILIP

And afterwards you killed my troops with thirst,
Following a crazy scheme which overbore you.

Don John

Not crazy, unsuccessful.

Philip

Poor vain ghost,
Poor flickering candle that was bright awhile.

Don John

I was the man whom Europe worshipped most,
One with a mighty plan which you thought guile.
Why did you kill me, Philip?

Philip

You betrayed me,
Or would have, traitor, had I not been wise.

Don John

I was your board's best piece, you should have played me,
Now I am dead and earth is in my eyes.
I could have won you England. I had planned
To conquer England. I had all prepared
Ships, soldiers, money, but your cruel hand
Killed me, and nothing's done and nothing's dared.

Philip

You planned to conquer England and be King;
Those who obstruct my path I sweep aside.

Don John

Brother, there is a time for everything;
That was the time for England, but I died;
Now you attempt too late,
The powers have closed the gate,
Destiny enters by another door,
The lost chance comes no more.

The Voice of Escovedo

Philip, he tells the truth. We could have won
England for you, we were no plotters then.

Voices

Philip, you were betrayed, you were undone.
You had the moment, but you killed the men.

Escovedo

The liar, Perez, tricked you.   O great King!
We would have added England to your crown,
Now the worms cling
About our lips deep down.
You had me stabbed at midnight going home
That man of Perez' stabbed me in the back.
And then I could not stir, down on the loam;
The sky was full of blood, the stars were black.
And then I knew my wife and children waited
But that I could not come; a moving hand
Had interposed a something fated
'Twixt us and what we planned.

Don John

You had me poisoned in that Holland den,
Outcast, alone, without the help of men.
We planned a glorious hour
Hoisting the banner of Spain
On the top of London Tower,
With England a Spanish fief.
Life cannot happen again,
And doing dies with the brain;
Autumn ruins the flower
And after the flower the leaf.

Voices

Philip, Philip, Philip!
The evil men do has strength,
It gathers behind the veils
While the unjust thing prevails.
While the pride of life is strong,

But the balance tips at length,
And the unjust things are tales,
The pride of life is a song.

PHILIP

I kept my purpose while you lived. Shall I
Be weaker, now that you are dead, you things?
What can such reedy wretches do but die
Standing against the purposes of Kings?

DON JOHN

Do? We can thwart you.

VOICES

And we will, we will;
All Spain's unjustly murdered work you ill.
Gather against him, gather, mock him down.

THE VOICE OF THE MARQUIS OF SANTA CRUZ

Scatter, you shadows, fly. Philip, great King.
You vultures gathered in an unclean ring;
Away, you shadows, scatter.
They are gone,

[*The* MARQUIS *enters*]

PHILIP

Who calls?

SANTA CRUZ

Master.

PHILIP

Let me dream on.
Whose voice was that? It warned me of defeat.

SANTA CRUZ

I am that Santa Cruz who built your fleet,
And died to make it good. It was my child.
I call because my work has been defiled.

Philip

Why rail, uneasy soul?

Santa Cruz

If I had spent
Less life in that, I should be still alive,
Commanding what I built to my content,
Driving the English slaves as conquerors drive.
Why did you give away my splendid sword,
Forged by a never-conquered captain's brain,
Into the hoof-hand of an ambling lord,
Useless in all things, but to ruin Spain?
Would God I had but guessed it! Would my stars
Had shown me clearer what my death would bring,
I would have burned those galleons, guns and spars,
Soldiers and all, and so have stopped this thing.
And doing that I should have served you well,
And brought less ruin on this lovely land.
What folly from the unfed brain of hell
Made you promote that thing to my command?—
Folly from which so many men must die.

Philip

We stand against all comers, Time and I.
I chose the Duke because I wanted one . . .
Who . . .

Santa Cruz

Give no reason for the evil done.
Souls wrestle from the ever deedless grave
To do, not to hear reason. Oh, great King,
You still may save the ruin of this thing!

Philip

You speak of ruin. Tell me what you see.

Santa Cruz

Ruin that threatens, but need never be.

Be silent, Philip; listen while I tell
What you must do.

PHILIP

You are a voice from hell;
I will not listen to these obscene dreams.

SANTA CRUZ

Life is a heavy cloud, through which come gleams.
Oh, Philip, let me speak! Philip, I say,
One way can still be tried; I see the way.
You must do this, but listen.

PHILIP

I still doubt.

SANTA CRUZ

Listen, great King; the light is dying out.
You are fading from me, Philip; they are coming.
Before it is too late for ever send . . .

PHILIP

Send?

SANTA CRUZ

Yes.

PHILIP

To whom?

SANTA CRUZ

To . . .

VOICES

Drown his voice with drumming;
Pipe with the Inca conch, the Indian flute.
What red flowers spring from this blood-sprinkled root!

PHILIP

What name was that you said?

SANTA CRUZ

Wait, Philip—wait;
They are so many and so full of hate.

VOICES

Call to your monarch, Marquis—call again.

PHILIP

Something he meant is knocking at my brain—
Knocking for entrance.   Marquis!

SANTA CRUZ

Philip!   King!

PHILIP

What must I do?

SANTA CRUZ

Oh, fiends!

VOICES

Ah, conquerors, sing!
Now we have triumphed.
     We have torn the flag.
Dance in a ring, victorious spirits, dance;
Brought to a byword is the Spanish brag.
And ruined is the grand inheritance.
Mourn, wretched Philip, for your plans are checked;
Your colonies defenceless; your sweet faith
Mocked by the heretics; your ships are wrecked;
The strength of Spain has dwindled to a wraith.
Aha! you beaten King, you blinded fool!
Scream, for the empire tumbles from your rule.

PHILIP

God will deliver me; you are but words
Called in the night-time by malignant birds
But who are you?

[*The figure of* DE LEYVA *enters*]

Voice of De Leyva

I am De Leyva, come
Out of the sea, my everlasting home,
To whisper comfort to my ruined friend.
Dear, I am dead, but friendship cannot end;
Love does not die, and I am with you here.
Often in sorrow you will feel me near,
Feel me, but never speak, nor hear me speak.
Philip, whatever bitter Fate may wreak
On Spain and you, remember I am here,
The dead are bound to those they held most dear.

Philip

Dreams of the night.   I dreamed De Leyva came.

Voices

Awake to hear the story of your shame.

[*They cry.   A gun is shot off.   Bells*]

Philip

[*Rousing.*]   I dreamed I was defeated like those men
Whom I defeated; I have felt their woe.
What is this noise?   A message?

Enter then.

Princess

A prisoner comes with news of victory.

Philip

So.
Victory comes!   We win!

Princess

The fleet has won!

Philip

Thanks be to God on high.

Princess

His will be done.

PHILIP

Lord, help me use this victory for Thy praise.
Lord, Thou hast burst this night of many days
With glorious morning and my heart is full.
O God, my God, Thy ways are wonderful!
Bring me the prisoner.

PRINCESS

He brought this letter.

[*An Englishman is brought in*]

PHILIP

You are an Englishman?

PRISONER

Yes, your Majesty.

PHILIP

This letter says that you can tell me how things have fared.
Tell me your story.

PRISONER

I was at sea, my lord, fishing, some fifteen miles south-west
from Falmouth. We were not expecting the Spanish fleet, our
cruisers had said it was not coming. It was hazy summer
weather and early morning. We could hear that we were
among a big fleet, and when the haze lifted your ships were
all round us, so we were taken aboard an admiral's ship. A
dark man the admiral was, with a very quick way; he was
not the chief admiral, but an Admiral Recalde, with the rear-
guard.

PHILIP

Where was the English fleet at that time? Was it expecting us?

PRISONER

No, your honour. It was windbound in Plymouth, unpre-
pared, as I told your admiral. Then I was taken down below.

PHILIP

Did our fleet enter Plymouth, then?

PRISONER

No, my lord, and I could not think why, for the wind held and they had only to sail straight in. The day passed.

The next day there was firing, and I thought "The English have got out of the trap at least," but the firing died down, and I concluded the English were beaten.

PHILIP

Yes?

PRISONER

I thought the ships would put ashore then to take what they had won, but they kept at sea some days, though there was firing every day, sometimes very heavy. They said they were burning all the English towns as they passed, and then going to France to fetch an army; and after some nights I was brought ashore in Calais to come to your Majesty.

PHILIP

What did you see in Calais?

PRISONER

It was a dark night, my lord, when they sent me in. I saw the road full of shipping, lit up like a town.

PHILIP

What was the feeling among you English prisoners? That the Spaniards had prospered?

PRISONER

Yes, my lord. You had reached your army, which was all your intent. You had only to take it across the Channel; the wind was fair for that.

PHILIP

So then you started for Spain. You know no more of what happened?

PRISONER

No, my lord, except that looking back from a hilltop, I saw a great glare over Calais.

PHILIP

Something was burning there?

PRISONER

It was the bonfires, my lord, to give them light; they were embarking the army. Then in France later on we heard that Drake had been sunk off Calais with fifteen ships. A man said he had seen it. That is all I know, my lord.

PHILIP

What you say will be proved. You will be returned to England. Treat this man well. [*Exit* PRISONER.]

PRINCESS

Father, what blessed news!

PHILIP

             We have not failed;
But then he hardly knew. The letter here
Shows that our navy partly has prevailed.

PRINCESS

The news has spread.

CRIES WITHOUT

         Long live King Philip! Cheer!

CRIES

Cheer our great King! Long live our noble King.
Beat "Santiago," drummers.

PRINCESS

Hark! they sing.
The court is dark with people, but more come.

CRIES

Long live King Philip!

A GREAT VOICE

Silence for the drum!
And when the drum beats, we will lift our thanks
Till his heart triumphs.

Silence in the ranks!
Eyes front! O people, listen! Our attempt
Has triumphed more than our desires dreamt.
England is ours. Give thanks. Sound trumpets. Sing!

CRIES

Philip, Philip the King! God save the King!
Philip the conqueror! Philip! [*A strange cry.*]

PRINCESS

Oh, look! look! . . .
Just as they cheered, the palace banners shook,
They took it for a sign.

The guards are there,
Look, and the monks are forming in the square
Bringing the blessed relics. Oh, my dear!
I am so happy. Listen how they cheer.
Father, they're cheering because Spain has won.
All you have hoped and striven for is done.
I hardly dare believe it.

CRIES

Long live Spain.

PRINCESS

O, there are horsemen, I must look again!

CRIES

There is the Princess at the window.   See?
God save you, little lady.   Which is she?
There.   Is the King there?   He must be.   Yes.
God save your Grace.   He's there with the Princess.

PHILIP

Stand farther back; they saw you.

PRINCESS

                         Oh, not now!
They called "God save me," father; let me bow.

PHILIP

Bow, then, my dear.

CRIES

               God save your pretty face.

PRINCESS

Father, do come, they want you.

CRIES

               Bless your Grace.
God save the King—King Philip.

PRINCESS

               Father dear,
They're calling for you; stand beside me here.

PHILIP

Not yet.   It is not time.

CRIES

Philip the King!

PRINCESS

Oh, father, come!   It is a thrilling thing
To know they won, and hear these shouts of praise.

CRIES

God save the King! God send him many days!
Philip the King, the conqueror of the sea!
St. James for Spain, King Philip, victory!
King Philip! Santiago!

PRINCESS

Father.

PHILIP

Wait!
Kings must not yield them at too cheap a rate.

VOICES

Philip the King! The English are destroyed!
God save him! Victory! We are overjoyed!
Let the bells ring! King Philip! Philip! King!
Ring the Cathedral bells—ay, let them ring!
St. James for Spain! King Philip! Clear the guns!

[Guns shot off]

King Philip, fire—fire all at once.
King Philip, fire! King Philip, fire! St. James!
Thank God, the King of kings, the Name of names!
Fire, King Philip! Santiago, fire!
Give thanks to God who gives us our desire!
Philip, God save and bless him!

PHILIP

[Going to window]

I will speak.

VOICES

Fire! He's there! King Philip!

PHILIP

Man is weak.

VOICES

He's there!

PRINCESS

Oh, father, look!

PHILIP

             Stand at my side.

VOICES

God bless and guard our blessed country's guide!
King Philip, fire! The King! [*The bells begin.*]

PRINCESS

            Oh, bells of joy!
And now the monks are singing.

THE MONKS

Let us give thanks unto the Lord of lords,
Who saves His faithful from the Egyptian swords.

VOICES

Amen. God save the King.

THE MONKS

He made the Red Sea waters to divide,
And led our Israel through with Him for guide.

VOICES

Amen. God save the King! Philip the King!

PHILIP

O God, I thank Thee for this marvellous thing.

THE MONKS

He whelmed King Pharaoh's army in the sea,
And of His mercy gave us victory.

Voices

The famous kings are blown like chaff
Before Thy fiery car.
Thou smit'st th' ungodly with Thy staff . . .
Philip the King!   God save our prudent King!

Philip

My subjects, whom God gave me for His ends . . .

Princess

Whatever pain you bore, this makes amends.

Voices

Speak to your loving hearts, your Majesty.

Philip

I do His will; to God the glory be.

The Monks

Praise Him, O sun and moon, morning and evening star!
The kings who mocked His word are broken in the war.
Praise Him with heart and soul!   Praise Him with voice and
    lute!

Voices

The King!   God save the King!   Silence!   He speaks.   Salute!

The Monks

In the dark night, ere dawn, we will arise and sing
Glory to God on high, the praises of our King.

Voices

The King is going to speak.   He makes a sign.
God bless your noble Grace and all your line!
God bless you, Sir, for all your thought for us!
The conquering King, Philip victorious!
Philip the great and good!   Hush!   Silence!   Peace!

Philip! Attention! Bid the ringers cease.
The King is going to speak; he raised his hand.

PRINCESS

Dear, to be loved as you are is most grand.
Speak to them, father; thank them for their love.

THE MONKS

I will exalt the Name of God above.

VOICES

The bells are hushed. Be quiet! Silence all!

PHILIP

I thought I heard, far off, a funeral call;
As in your dream, a melancholy cry.

PRINCESS

It was the fifes.

PHILIP

       No; listen!

PRINCESS

           That sound?

PHILIP

                   Ay.

PRINCESS

It was the crowd outside. Now they are still.

PHILIP

No, it was singing coming up the hill—
Sad singing, too.

PRINCESS

       I did not hear it.

PHILIP

            There!

PRINCESS

The bells have left a trembling in the air.

PHILIP

No; it was voices.   I will speak one word
To these below.   There is the noise I heard
        [RECALDE'S *men are heard singing*]

RECALDE'S MEN

Out of the deep, out of the deep, we come,
Preserved from death at sea to die at home.
Mercy of God alone preserved us thus;
In the waste sea Death laid his hand on us.

PRINCESS

The Black Monks in a penitential psalm.

VOICES

Philip the King!

PHILIP

      I'll wait.

PRINCESS

        Oh, speak!

PHILIP

               Be calm!
I cannot cross God's word with words of mine.

VOICES

Quiet, you singers!

PRINCESS

       They are men in line.
        [RECALDE'S *men are heard singing*]

RECALDE'S MEN

We called the world too small with boastful lips;
Now we are ghosts crawled from the bones of ships.

We were most glorious at our setting sail;
Now our knees knock, our broken spirits fail.
Our banner is abased and all our pride:
A tale of ships that sank and men who died.

PRINCESS

Listen! Who are they?

PHILIP

What is it they sing?

VOICES

The King is speaking.   Silence for the King!
Let the King speak; be still.   You ragged crew,
Have you no manners?   Silence!   Who are you?

RECALDE'S MEN

We are the beaten men, the men accursed,
Whose bitter glory 'tis t' have borne the worst.

PRINCESS

They are not monks.

PHILIP

Nor beggars.

PRINCESS

Now they stand.

VOICES

Yon navy's sweepings driven back to land.
Go to the hens and tunnies; beat them down
Back to the sea you ran from; back and drown.

RECALDE'S MEN

Pity our shame, you untried heroes here.
Defeat's not victory, but 'tis bought as dear.

PHILIP

They are sailors from the fleet.

PRINCESS

They come with news.
They are ragged to the skin, they have no shoes.

PHILIP

The crowd is still.

PRINCESS

Why do they come like this?

PHILIP

Listen; their Captain tells them what it is.

RECALDE'S MEN

Darken the bedrooms for us, people all,
And let us turn our faces to the wall,
And let the darkness and the silence make
A quiet time in which our hearts may break.

[*A murmur runs through the Court*]

PRINCESS

Father, what is it?

PHILIP

Child, the Act of One
Who chastens earthly kings, whose Will be done.

PRINCESS

It means that we are beaten?

PHILIP

Who can tell?

PRINCESS

Father.

PHILIP

Dear child, even defeat is well.

PRINCESS

I thought that we were happy.

PHILIP

                      Watch the square.
Now tell me calmly what is passing there.

PRINCESS

The Captain comes, the crowd is making way.

PHILIP

Who is it? Can you see?

PRINCESS

                   His hair is grey.
He walks bareheaded, slowly, and the crowd
Shrink as though Death were passing in his shroud.

PHILIP

Worse news has come. Who is the man?

PRINCESS

His face . . .
I seem to know him, but the air is strange.
He puts the touch of Death upon the place.
Nothing but Death could fashion such a change.
He carries something. Now the people kneel.
We are defeated, Father.

PHILIP

                  What I feel
I cover. Go within. Misfortune stuns
None but the tender.   [*Exit* PRINCESS.]

VOICES

            Give us back our sons.
Philip, give back our sons, our lovely sons.

THE PALACE GUARD

Halt! Who comes there?

A VOICE

            Spain and the Empire.

The Guard

Pass,

Spain and the Empire.

Voices

They are drowned. Alas!
Philip, give back our sons, our lovely sons.

[*Enter* MESSENGER, *carrying an Admiral's chain*]

Philip

What brings you to me, Captain?

Messenger

This gold chain . . .
Bears the twelve badges of the strength of Spain
Once linked in glory, Philip, but now loosed.

[*Detaching link from link*]

Castilla, Leon, Aragon, and these,
Palestine, Portugal, the Sicilies,
Navarre, Granada, the Valencian State,
The Indies, East and West, the Archducate,
The Western Mainland in the Ocean Sea.
Those who upheld their strength have ceased to be.
I, who am dying, King, have seen their graves.
Philip, your Navy is beneath the waves.

Philip

He who in bounty gives in wisdom takes.

Messenger

O King, forgive me, for my spirit breaks;
I saw those beaches where the Grange descends
White with unburied corpses of stripped friends.

Philip

I grieve that Spain's disaster brings such loss.

MESSENGER

From Pentland to the Groyne the tempests toss
Unshriven Spaniards driving with the tide.
They were my lovely friends and they have died,
Far from wind-broken Biscay, far from home,
With no anointing chrism but the foam.

PHILIP

The dead will rise from unsuspected slime;
God's chosen will be gathered in God's time.

MESSENGER

King, they died helpless; our unwieldy fleet
Made such a target to the English guns
That we were riddled through like sifted wheat.
We never came to grappling with them once.
They raked us from a distance, and then ran.
Each village throughout Spain has lost a man;
The widows in the seaports fill the streets.

PHILIP

Uncertain chance decides the fate of fleets.

MESSENGER

Now the North Sea is haunted for all time
By miserable souls whose dying words
Cursed the too proud adventure as a crime.
Our broken galleons house the gannet-birds.
The Irish burn our Captains' bones for lime.
O misery that the might of England wrought!

PHILIP

Christ is the only remedy for thought
When the mind sickens.   We are pieces played,
Not moving as we will, but as we are made;
Beaten and spurred at times like stubborn steeds,

That we may go God's way.   Your spirit bleeds,
Having been proved in trouble past her strength.
Give me the roll in all its ghastly length.
Which of my friends survive, if any live?

MESSENGER

Some have survived, but all are fugitive.
Your Admiral in command is living still;
Michael Oquendo too, though he is ill,
Dying of broken heart and bitter shame.
Valdes is prisoner, Manrique the same.

PHILIP

God willed the matter; they are not to blame.
Thank God that they are living.   Name the rest.

MESSENGER

They are all dead . . . with him you loved the best.

PHILIP

I dreamed De Leyva died, so it is true?

MESSENGER

Drowned on the Irish coast with all his crew.
After enduring dying many days
The sea has given him quiet. Many ways
Lead men to death, and he a hard one trod,
Bearing much misery, like a knight of God.

PHILIP

Amen.   Go on.

MESSENGER

Hugh de Moncada died,
Shot in his burning ship by Calais side,
Cheering his men to save her.   Pimentel
Sank in a galleon shambled like a hell
Rather than yield, and in a whirl of flames

Pedro Mendoza, Captain of St. James,
Stood with Don Philip thrusting boarders back
Till their Toledan armour was burnt black,
And both their helms ran blood.   And there they fell,
Shot down to bleed to death.   They perished well,
Happy to die in battle for their King
Before defeat had fallen on their friends;
Happier than most, for where the merrows sing
Paredes and his brother met their ends,
And Don Alarcon, cast alive ashore,
Was killed and stripped and hanged upon a tree.
And young Mendoza, whom the flagship bore,
Died of starvation and of misery.
But hundreds perished, King; why mention these?
Battle and hunger, heart-break, and the seas
Have overwhelmed the chivalry of Spain.

Philip

Misfortune, after effort, brings no stain.
Perhaps I underjudged the English fleet.
How was it that the Spaniards met defeat?
What evil fortune brought about our fall?

Messenger

Their sailors and their cannon did it all.

Philip

Yet when the fleet reached Calais all went well.

Messenger

Our woes began there.

Philip

Tell me what befell.

Messenger

We were to ship the troops in Calais Road;
They lay encamped, prepared to go aboard.

To windward still the English fleet abode—
Still as in port when peace has been restored.

>The wind and sea were fair,
>We lay at anchor there;
>The stars burned in the air,
>The men were sleeping,
>When in the midnight dark
>Our watchman saw a spark
>Suddenly light a bark
>With long flames leaping.

>Then, as they stood amazed,
>Others and others blazed;
>Then terror set them crazed,
>They ran down screaming:
>"Fire-ships are coming! Wake
>Cast loose, for Jesus' sake!
>Eight fire-ships come from Drake—
>Look at their gleaming!"

>Roused in the dark from bed,
>We saw the fire show red,
>And instant panic spread
>Through troops and sailors;
>They swarmed on deck unclad,
>They did what terror bade,
>King, they were like the mad
>Escaped from jailers.

>Some prayed for mercy, some
>Rang bells or beat the drum,
>As though despair had come
>At hell's contriving;
>Captains with terror pale
>Screamed through the dark their hail,

"Cut cable, loose the sail,
  And set all driving!"

Heading all ways at once,
Grinding each other's guns,
Our blundering galleons
Athwart-hawse galleys,
Timbers and plankings cleft,
And half our tackling reft,
Your grand Armada left
The roads of Calais.

Weary and overwrought
We strove to make all taut;
But when the morning brought
The dawn to light us,
Drake, with the weather gage,
Made signal to engage,
And, like a pard in rage,
Bore down to fight us.

Nobly the English line
Trampled the bubbled brine;
We heard the gun-trucks whine
To the taut laniard.
Onwards we saw them forge,
White billowing at the gorge.
"On, on!" they cried, "St. George!
Down with the Spaniard!"

From their van squadron broke
A withering battle-stroke,
Tearing our plankèd oak
By straiks asunder,
Blasting the wood like rot
With such a hail of shot,

So constant and so hot
It beat us under.

The English would not close;
They fought us as they chose,
Dealing us deadly blows
For seven hours.
Lords of our chiefest rank
The bitter billow drank,
For there the English sank
Three ships of ours.

*   *   *   *   *   *

Then the wind forced us northward from the fight;
We could not ship the army nor return;
We held the sea in trouble through the night,
Watching the English signals blink and burn.
The English in a dim cloud kept astern;
All night they signalled, while our shattered ships
Huddled like beasts beneath the drovers' whips.

*   *   *   *   *   *

At dawn the same wind held; we could not strive.
The English drove us north as herdsmen drive.

*   *   *   *   *   *

Under our tattered flags,
With rigging cut to rags,
Our ships like stricken stags
Were heaped and hounded,
Caught by the unknown tide,
With neither chart nor guide,
We fouled the Holland side,
Where four more grounded.

Our water-casks were burst,
The horses died of thirst,

The wounded raved and curst,
Uncared, untended.
All night we heard the crying
Of lonely shipmates dying;
We had to leave them lying
So the fight ended.

PHILIP

God gives His victory as He wills.   But this
Was not complete destruction.   What thing worse
Came to destroy you?

MESSENGER

An avenging curse,
Due for old sins, destroyed us.

PHILIP

Tell the tale.

MESSENGER

O King, when morning dawned it blew a gale,
But still the English followed, and we fled
Till breakers made the dirty waters pale.
We saw the Zealand sandbanks right ahead,
Blind in a whirling spray that gave us dread;
For we were blown there, and the water shoaled.
The crying of the leadsmen at the lead,
Calling the soundings, were our death-bells tolled.

We drifted down to death upon the sands—
The English drew away to watch us drown;
We saw the bitter breakers with grey hands
Tear the dead body of the sandbank brown.
We could do nothing, so we drifted down
Singing the psalms for death—we who had been
Lords of the sea and knights of great renown,
Doomed to be strangled by a death unclean.

PHILIP

So there the ships were wrecked?

MESSENGER

      Time had not struck.
O King, we learned how blessed mercy saves:
Even as our forefoot grounded on the muck,
Tripping us up to drown us in the waves,
A sudden windshift snatched us from our graves
And drove us north; and now another woe,
Tempest unending, beat our ships to staves—
A never-dying gale with frost and snow.

Now our hearts failed, for food and water failed;
The men fell sick by troops, the wounded died.
They washed about the wet decks as we sailed
For want of strength to lift them overside.
Desolate seas we sailed, so grim, so wide,
That ship by ship our comrades disappeared.
With neither sun nor star to be a guide,
Like spirits of the wretched dead we steered.

Till, having beaten through the Pentland Pass,
We saw the Irish surf, with mists of spray
Blowing far inland, blasting trees and grass,
And gave God thanks, for we espied a bay
Safe, with bright water running down the clay—
A running brook where we could drink and drink.
But drawing near, our ships were cast away,
Bilged on the rocks; we saw our comrades sink . . .

Or worse: for those the breakers cast ashore
The Irish killed and stripped; their bodies white
Lay naked to the wolves—yea, sixty score—
All down the windy beach, a piteous sight.
The savage Irish watched by bonfire light
Lest more should come ashore; we heard them there

Screaming the bloody news of their delight.
Then we abandoned hope and knew despair.

And now the fleet is sunken in the sea,
And all the seamen, all the might of Spain,
Are dead, O King, and out of misery,
Never to drag at frozen ropes again—
Never to know defeat, nor feel the pain
Of watching dear companions sink and die.
Death's everlasting armistice to the brain
Gives their poor griefs quietus; let them lie.

I, like a ghost returning from the grave,
Come from a stricken ship to tell the news
Of Spanish honour which we could not save,
Nor win again, nor even die to lose;
And since God's hidden wisdom loves to bruise
Those whom he loves, we, trembling in despair,
Will watch our griefs to see God's finger there,
And make His will our solace and excuse.

Defeat is bitter and the truth is hard—
Spain is defeated, England has prevailed;
This is the banner which I could not guard,
And this the consecrated sword which failed.
Do with your dying Captain as you will.

[He lays down sword and banner]

PHILIP

I, from my heart, thank God, from whose great hand
I am so helped with power, I can still
Set out another fleet against that land.
Nor do I think it ill
If all the running water takes its course
While there are unspent fountains at the source.

He sendeth out His word and melteth them.
Take back your standard, Captain.   As you go,
Bid the bells toll and let the clergy come.
Then in the city by the strike of drum
Proclaim a general fast.   In bitter days
The soul finds God, God us.

[Exit CAPTAIN]

PHILIP

[Alone]

De Leyva, friend,
Whom I shall never see, never again,
This misery that I feel is over Spain.
O God, beloved God, in pity send
That blessed rose among the thorns—an end:
Give a bruised spirit peace.

[He kneels.   A muffled march of the drums]

CURTAIN

ESTHER AND BERENICE

Two Plays

PREFACE

I have been asked to write a few words to explain why these adaptations of Racine were made.

They were made for the use of a little company of amateur players who wished to try their art in verse plays, yet found that of the many fine poetical plays in the English language, not many suited their needs. The Elizabethan poetical play needs a large cast and a fairly large stage. The Restoration poetical play is of an old fashion. The modern poetical play is usually not enough of the stage nor of the people to hold the audience to which these players perform.

The stage upon which this company of players performs measures eleven feet by thirteen feet, so that no big production is possible. The men players are often kept from performing by their work or study, so that no play with a large man cast can be undertaken. We had produced some half dozen plays of different kinds, and had learned that the poetical plays were by much the most popular. We wanted to do others. We wanted, in short, plays in verse that were of the theatre, that could be done with few properties and no scenery, with small casts of from six to nine persons. Knowing how keenly sensitive an English audience is to verse, we wanted plays with fine situations and stirring declamation. The Frence classical tragedies seemed to offer a foundation of what we needed, so these versions were made.

The play of *Esther* is an adaptation, not a translation, because in *Esther* our audience asked for something more than the French formality allowed. We could make nothing of Racine's choruses in this play in translation; after some attempts we gave them up, and substituted others. When we came to rehearse the play, we found it too short; we therefore lengthened it. *Berenice* is a translation.

JOHN MASEFIELD.

This adaptation of "Esther" was produced by Miss Penelope Wheeler at Wootton, Berks, on the evening of the 5th May, 1921, with the following cast:—

ESTHER.....................Miss Penelope Wheeler
RACHEL.....................Miss Geraldine Berkeley
MORDECAI...................Mr. Richard Elwes
HAMAN......................Mr. Kenneth Rae
HYDASPES...................Mr. W. H. Nurse
AHASUERUS..................Mr. Eric Dance
ASAPH......................Mr. James Pearce
ZERESH.....................Mrs. Vidler
CHORUS.................... { Miss Katharine Richards
                          { Miss Judith Masefield
GUARD......................Mr. P. Venables
GHOST OF THARES...........

The Play was performed without scenery upon a stage hung with curtains. There were exits and entrances R. and L. at Back, and an extra exit and approach by steps to the stage from Front Centre.

ESTHER

CHARACTERS

ESTHER
RACHEL
MORDECAI
HAMAN

HYDASPES
AHASUERUS
ASAPH
ZERESH

CHORUS OF JEWISH CHILDREN
GUARDS, ETC.

Parts of Acts 1, 3, and 4 of this play are translated from the Tragedy of Esther, by Racine.

PROPERTIES

ACT I

Settle with cushions, to Left.
Seats for CHORUS, Left, with rug.
Orders for MORDECAI, Right.

ACT II

Couch R. for AHASUERUS, with cushions and cover.
Sword at foot of bed.
Stool at foot of bed.
Cup for drink, Left, off.
Bell for clink, Right, off.
Drum, Left, off, with the GUARDS, for their singing.
Battens to keep couch steady.

ACT III

Settle, bedecked, to the Right, with new covers and cushions, as the throne.
Sceptre, AHASUERUS, Right.
Roll or scroll, AHASUERUS, Right.
Spear for GUARD, Right.

ACT IV

Throne, bedecked as in Act III, but Centre.
Fruit and two brass dishes for feast (oranges and lemons only).
Bronze bowls and cups for feast.
Stool for feast.
Orders, Right, off, for AHASUERUS, when he goes out.
Second stool or footstool to Right of throne.
Signet for ASAPH to give to the King, Right.

ESTHER

ACT I

SCENE:—ESTHER'S *apartments*.
(RACHEL *enters back, comes down L. of* ESTHER.)

ESTHER

O Rachel, is it you? Thrice happy day,
O blessed heaven, which sends you to my prayers.
You did not know that I was made the Queen?
More than six months my friends have sought for you.
Where have you been?

(*They sit Centre.*)

RACHEL

I heard that you were dead,
And hearing this, I lived most miserably,
Until a prophet told me, "Do not weep,
But rise, leave this, and take the Shushan road;
There you will see your Esther crowned the Queen.
And on your way comfort the wretched tribes;
Tell them the day approaches when our God
Will send His comfort with a powerful arm."
I heard his words, and hurried to the palace.
Marvellous it is that proud Ahasuerus
Has crowned his captive, made a *Jewess* Queen.
O by what hidden ways, what strange events,
Has Heaven led you to this great position?

ESTHER

Have they not told you of the great disgrace
Of the proud Vashti, Queen before my coming?
The King divorced her, but when she was gone
His mind was troubled, and he sought for one

To bring him comfort.
They sought throughout the world in every land
To find a Queen.
I, as an orphan, lived alone and hidden
Under the care of watchful Mordecai:
He is my uncle, and he tended me.
Sad for the trouble of the captive Jews,
He told me all his secret plans, and I
Obeyed his wish, and sought to be the Queen.
Who could express the plots and counter-plots
Of all these courtiers, striving for the honour,
Striving to catch Ahasuerus' eyes.
At last Ahasuerus' order came to me,
And I appeared before the mighty King.
Long time he watched me in a sombre silence,
Then gently spoke: "You shall be Queen," he said,
And crowned me with his royal diadem.
Then followed days of joys and festivals;
Esther was Queen, and seated in the purple;
Half of the world was subject to her sceptre.
But grass is growing in Jerusalem,
The stones are scattered from the holy Temple,
The God of Israel's worship is no more.

RACHEL

Have you not told the King your troubles, Esther?

ESTHER

The King?   Even now he knows not that I am a Jewess,
For Mordecai keeps me secret still.

RACHEL

Can Mordecai come about the Court?

ESTHER

His love for me finds out a thousand ways

To send advice, and me to ask for it.
A Father has less care for his own son.
Already by good Mordecai's cunning
I have laid bare to the King the treacherous plots
Made by two slaves against him.
Meanwhile my love for our beloved race
Has filled this palace with young Jewesses.
Here I can care for them and teach their souls.
Among them, putting by my queenly pride,
I bow myself before the feet of God;
I hide from all the Persians who they are.
(*Calls.*) Come! Come, my daughters,
Companions here of my captivity.

(*Enter* CHORUS, *Left: bow slightly, and come down to front Left.
They stand and speak standing.*)

RACHEL

Innocent children, may God give you peace.

ESTHER

My daughters, sing us one of those sweet psalms
That tell of Zion.

1ST CHORUS

We cannot sing of Zion without tears.

2ND CHORUS

How can we sing the happy songs of home
In this strange land?

1ST CHORUS

All day and every **day**
The memory of old pleasure comes to us,
Old happy days at home with father and mother,
Our games and birthday feasts, and times at night
When lamps were lit.

Rachel

It is too true; their hearts are breaking, Esther.
We exiled captives cannot sing of home.

Esther

Sing of the war, and our captivity.

1st Chorus

The fulness of our hearts is all we have,
We can sing that.

1st Chorus

A myriad Persians came against our town,
  Many in number as the blades of grass:
They broke the ramparts of the city down,
  They robbed our Temple of its wealth of brass.

They made the captains of our soldiers yield,
  They took our Kings and Princes captive there,
They blinded them, and killed them in the field,
  They made us slaves: they gave us loads to bear.

Then, on a day, the Persian trumpets sounded;
  They brought us from the city.   Even as a beast
Bearing a too great burden, we were hounded
  Far from our home away into the East.

And, looking back, even as we topped a rise,
  We saw, far, far behind, our ruined city
Burning, a spoil to warriors without pity,
  And we, the homeless slaves, the warriors' prize.

2nd Chorus

Now many a day has passed, and here as slaves
  We toil, with breaking hearts, by tears made blind;
Thinking of our old homes, our fathers' graves,
  Lost, like our chance of life, our peace of mind.

Now no foot falls in the houses of our fathers,
   But the grass grows green and the fountain pipes are filled
With the ashes, and the ruin, and the burnt-out rafters,
   And where once our Kings caroused the sparrows build.

(*Enter* MORDECAI, *Right. He comes down below* RACHEL. *He has his face hidden.*)

ESTHER

What profane man dares come into this place?
O Mordecai! Uncle! Is it you?
An angel of the Lord has helped you here.
But why so sad?
Why are you wearing sackcloth
All strewn with ashes?

MORDECAI

O wretched Queen!

(*He turns away from Queen.*)

O ghastly fortune of the innocent Jews!
Read, read the awful order that condemns us.
We are all lost, all ruined.

(RACHEL *down to* CHORUS *behind* ESTHER.)

ESTHER

O Heaven! my blood is frozen in my veins!

MORDECAI

They are about to massacre the Jews.
All of the Jewish nation is condemned.
Haman, the great King's favourite, plotted this;
The King, believing him, has signed the edict.
He gives his orders and in all his lands
To-morrow is appointed for our murder.

(*Alarm in* CHORUS.)

None of us will be spared, nor sex, nor age,
All of us will be killed and cast aside.

At the fifth hour to-morrow afternoon
The murder will begin.

ESTHER

O Heaven who sees such plots,
Hast thou forgotten us?

RACHEL

Heaven, who can guard us if thou dost not guard?

MORDECAI

Now, Esther, leave all weeping to these children;
You are our only hope, and you must save us.
The time is short and all of us are doomed;
You must go forth and dare to tell the King
That you yourself are Jewish.

ESTHER

Alas! you do not know what awful laws
Keep timid mortals from the awful King.
Death is the doom of any daring soul
Who comes before the King, not being bidden,
Unless the King think fit to stretch his sceptre
For him to kiss.
All living souls are subject to this law,
Even I, his Queen, am subject to this law.
If I his Queen desire to speak with him,
He must first call for me,
Or send for me.

MORDECAI

What! when you see your country at death's door,
Is your own life so blessed to you, Esther?
Is not your life due to the Jewish race,
Or due to God Who gave it?
Who knows, if to the throne you bend your steps
To save the Jews, God may protect you there.
O happy you, to risk your life for God!

The God Who vanquishes the kings of earth,
At Whose great Voice the sea flies, the sky trembles.
If He permitted Haman's wicked plot,
Doubtless it was to prove your holy zeal.
O He will vanquish Haman, break our chains,
By the most weak hand in His universe
And you, if you do not accept this deed,
Will die with all your race.

(CHORUS *hands out in entreaty to* ESTHER.)

ESTHER

If I accept the deed
And if I see the King and live to tell him
That I am Jewish, he will surely kill me
For having kept it secret until now.

MORDECAI

You could not have been Queen had it been known.
I bade you keep the secret for that reason;
Rightly, I judged it then.

ESTHER

But it proves wrongly,
It ruins our last hope.

MORDECAI

It is a hope,
Our only hope, and you must do it, Esther.

ESTHER

O God, Thou seest the spears that ring us in!

RACHEL

Esther, dear friend, for these sweet children's sakes
Dare do this deed. Think, Esther; but for you
Their tender limbs will pasture the wild beasts,
And these most innocent lips that sing God's praise

Be silenced, and our Zion desolate ever.
O I beseech you, hasten to the King!

The Chorus

Save us, great Queen!   Beseech the King to save us!

Esther

Go! let the Jews in Shushan pray for me,
And watch all night, and keep a solemn fast.
Now it is night; to-morrow at the dawn,
Contented well to die, if die I must,
I'll go, and offer me in sacrifice.

(*They veil.*   Mordecai *out here.*)

O sovereign Lord, kept here among the pagans,
Thou knowest how I loathe their heathen rites;
Thou knowest that this crown, which I must wear
In solemn feasts, I spurn beneath my feet
When I'm alone, preferring ashes to it.
O Lord, I waited for Thy word to come.
Now has the moment come, and I obey;
I go to dare to stand before the King.
It is for Thee I go; Lord, come with me,
To this fierce lion who knows not Thy law;
Grant that he be not angry, let me charm him;
Lord, turn his rage against our enemies.

(*During this speech* Esther *comes Right down to foot of stage.*)

1st Chorus

Deliver us from this threatened death, O heaven;
Out of this body of death in which we dwell,
O Spirit, set us free.

2nd Chorus

For here, as slaves,
We cannot sing thy praise, we cannot keep
Thy laws, but live in dread and in despair.

Rachel

We had the past. We lived once, long ago.
We do not live now, save in memory.
Now even that little penny-weight of life
Is grudged us, is not spared, is taken from us.

All

O lamentation, misery, woe, woe!

(Rachel *a little at back of* Chorus.)

Chorus

2nd Chorus

(*Spoken sitting.*)

In the troubled dreams a slave has ere I waken,
  I can see my city shining as of old,
  Roof and column of the Temple wreathed in gold;
And the ramparts proud as erst, before the town was taken,
  And the well-loved living shapes that now are cold.
Then I wake, a slave, and houseless and forsaken,
  Chained, an outcast, and a chattel, bought and sold.

1st Chorus

(*Sitting.*)

Now, for us, no future, but the corn-mill and the stranger
  In the foeman's house forever.
And the cold eyes of a master and the cruel eyes of danger,
  And the memory of joys returning never.

We who once were dainty ones and splendid,
  Now are slaves who grind the mill beneath a master's blow;
Would that when our fathers ended, we had ended,
  That we lay in Zion's soil, at peace with those.

All

O lamentation, misery, woe, woe!

1ST *and* 2ND CHORUS

(Together, standing.)

Here, from our prison gate, we see again
The never-ending sand, the Persian plain,
The long, long road, the stones that we should tread
Were we but free, to our beloved dead.

And in the Spring the birds fly to the west
  Over those deserts that the mountains hem,
They fly to our dear land; they fly to nest;
  We cannot go with them.

1ST CHORUS

(Standing.)

And in Springtime from the windows of the tower
  I can see the wild horses in the plain,
Treading stately but so lightly that they never break the flower,
  And they fade at speed to westward and they never come again.

2ND CHORUS

(Standing.)

And in Springtime at the quays the men of Tyre
  Set their ships towards the west and hoist their sail,
And our hearts cry "Take us with you to the land of our desire!"
And they hear our cry but will not take the crier:
  The crying of a slave can be of no avail.

TOGETHER

(Move at "Birds.")

Birds, horses, sailors, all are free to go
  To seek their homes beyond the wilderness;
But we, the homeless, only know

(1ST CHORUS *comes across Right below* ESTHER.   2ND CHORUS
     comes L., kneels at foot of ESTHER *Centre.*)

Weariful days of wearing-out distress.
  O lamentation, misery, woe, woe!

ESTHER, RACHEL AND THE REST
(Speaking in a group in Centre.)

Shall we be ever exiled, must it be
    That we must pass our days as slaves forever?
Far from our pleasant land, and never see
    Our sacred Hills and Jordan's blessed river.
Shall we not see again thy ramparts rise,
    O Zion, and thy splendid towers rebuilt,
And God's great Temple set for sacrifice
    By this our race, atoning for our guilt?
Or must our weary footsteps no more tread
The land we love, where those we loved are dead?

No, we shall see that lovely land no more
    Nor anything we loved there, place or friend,
Nor do, nor know, the things we hungered for.
    Like darts out of God's Hand our deaths descend
        To make an end.

Now we can crouch and pray and count the hours
    Until our murderers' feet are on the stair,
    And bright steel spurts the blood upon our hair
And lays us motionless among the flowers,
    White things that do not care.

And afterwards, who knows what moths we'll be
    Flying about the lamps of life at night
In death's great darkness, blindly, blunderingly.

The brook that sings i' the grass knows more delight,
    The ox that the men pole-axe has more peace
    Than prisoners' souls; but now there comes release—
We shall go home, to death, to-morrow night.

    O lamentation, misery, woe, woe!
              CURTAIN

ACT II

Ahasuerus

(Ahasuerus *on his couch.*)

What is the time?   I hear the water drip
Telling the time; and all the Court is still,
Still as the midnight; not a footstep stirs
Save the slow sentry on the palace wall.
No glow of light is in the eastern heaven;
The barren, dwindled moon her ruddy horn
Heaves o'er the tree-tops; it is midnight, sure.
I see Orion falling, and the Dog
Bright at his heels.   Deep midnight.   Not a sound
Save the most patient mouse that gnaws the wainscot.

(*He rises and walks.*)

O weary Time, I cannot sleep to-night.
All still, all sleep, save only I the King,
And that great city at the palace foot
Lies sleeping; yet a strange fear troubles me
That some there do not sleep, but prepare evil—
Evil against myself, against the King.
Those foreigners whom Haman told me of,
The Jews, who are to die, as Haman urged.
Excellent Haman, guardian of my throne.

It may be that his warning comes too late.
What if those Jews be coming even now
By the black alleys of that sleeping city
Into my palace, up the guarded stairs
From floor to floor, along the corridors,
Stealthily, with masked eyes, with bated breath,
On tiptoe to the threshold of my room.

That captain of my guard has eyed me strangely
These two nights now; he had an evil look.
He smiled, but still, his eyes: they did not smile.

Where is my sword? It's here. Look at that door.
It moved. Was that the wind? Who stands without?
I see you standing there. Come in there, you.
Who is it?

GUARD

(Off.)

The great King's guard is here.
God save the King! And may he live forever!

AHASUERUS

(Going Right back.)

Give me a cup of drink. I thirst. I thank you.
You men were sleeping when I called for you.
Sing, that I know you watching till I sleep.

(The SOLDIERS hum and sing together. AHASUERUS settles to
his sleep again. Count 20 slowly. Stop singing gradually.
He rouses up and walks again.)

There is a something evil in this room;
I seem to give it power by lying down.
It is as though the dark were full of souls
That wait till I am helpless and then come
Out of the corners, out of the air itself,
About my body; but, being up, they fly.

See, there is nothing here. I pass my hand—
(He goes round Right and Back feeling the walls.)
Here, here and here. I do not like that corner:
Is the thing there? The shadow on the wall
Is like the black head of an African
Thrown back in mockery, and it seems to move—
To move a little forward. It is but shadow.

(At Left Back.)

Yes, you are only shadow on the wall,
Not what you thought.

(He comes down stage.)

　　　　　　　　　　And yet I know this room
Is living with the spirits of evil things;
Spirits of evil things that I have done.
It is so difficult to be a King,
To wear the crown and to be ringed with death;
To order "Thus" with little time to think,
No time to know, but to be just, far-seeing,
Wise, generous, strict and yet most merciful,
As though one knew.

　　　　　　　　　　Now one by one they come,
Those plotters who defied me, whom I killed,
Crucified, burned, impaled, or tore with horses,
Men who with white lips cursed me, going to death.

　　　　　　　　　　　　　　(He turns facing Left.)

Yes, you pale ghosts, I mastered you in life,
And will in death.　I hold an Empire up,
A thing that IS; no glimmering dream of boys
Of what might be, but will not till men change;
No phantom Paradise of vengeance glutted
By poor men upon rich men, but a world
Rising and doing its work and lying down
Because my fierceness keeps the wolves at bay.
And yet, those Jews, even at my palace door,
So Haman said, have had my death contrived.
What if that captain be in league with them?
Guard!　Is Hydaspes there?

　　　　　　　　　　GUARD
He is here, great King.　Hydaspes, the King calls.

　　　　　　　　　　　　　　(HYDASPES *enters Left.*)
　　　　　　　　　　HYDASPES
Lord!　Do you call?

　　　　　　　　　　AHASUERUS.
Come in.　Let fall the hanging.　Come you there,

Into the moonlight, that I see your face.

                               *(*HYDASPES *comes down Left.*)*

Let me be sure that no one crawls behind you.
Hold out your hands, so; let me see the fingers.
Stay there.   No nearer.

                     You have travelled far?

HYDASPES

I have been far, among the Indian lands.

AHASUERUS

And saw strange peoples?

HYDASPES

                    Some.

AHASUERUS

Which were the strangest?

HYDASPES

Those of Tibet, who made their pence of gold,
And reckoned costly things by cups of water.

AHASUERUS

Who next seemed strange to you?

HYDASPES

                The Tartar horsemen
Who live on cheese of mare's milk, and go on
For ever over never-ending grass,
And have no home except the black felt tent
And the great plain and the great sky and silence.

AHASUERUS

A good life, that, for men.   Who, next to those?

HYDASPES

The race of Sittras by the sacred river;

They are all men, grown grey; no women there.
They have put by their wives and families,
Their crowns, their swords, their households and their cares,
And seek for wisdom there, until they die.

AHASUERUS

Do they find wisdom?

HYDASPES

No, but they find peace.

AHASUERUS

Do they, by Heaven; as a dead man does.
Wisdom is life upon the tickle edge.
Not the blind staring of the stupefied
At nothing out of nothing.   I envy you
For travelling thus and seeing all these things,
Which I shall only hear of.

Tell me now,
When you were wandering, did you meet the Jews?

HYDASPES

No, never, Lord.

AHASUERUS

Nor heard about their race?

HYDASPES

Not in the East.

AHASUERUS

But in the West you have?

HYDASPES

Yes, here at home.

AHASUERUS

What have you heard?

HYDASPES

That they are heathen men,

Brought from beyond the desert in the wars;
Not desert savages, nor civilized,
But enemies of both.

AHASUERUS

Who told you this?

HYDASPES

Prince Haman told me.

AHASUERUS

They are now condemned;
They have been plotting here.   You do not know
Any of their rebellious stock, by chance?

HYDASPES

No, Lord, not one.

AHASUERUS

Go to that door, Hydaspes.
Is someone listening to us, as we speak?

HYDASPES

(Going to door Left.)

No, Lord; the guard is at the door beyond.

AHASUERUS

Come nearer me.   That captain of the guard,
Is he a Jew?

HYDASPES

No, Lord, a Persian, surely,
Pordanatha, from lovely Arisai,
The city white like snow; Persian as you.

AHASUERUS

Thank you, Hydaspes.
These times are dangerous.   Go now from here,
See the guards doubled at Queen Esther's doors.
These Jews are secret like that desert tribe

Whom none has seen, who walk the moonless night
And strike men dead, and go, and leave no trace
Save the dead body.

HYDASPES

     I will place the guards
Myself, great King.

(Exit HYDASPES, Left.)

AHASUERUS

Esther, the Queen, not yet a trusted Queen.
Not lightly can an Emperor put his trust
In man or woman.   She is proud, and pride
Is slow to give or take in confidence.
How the Queen Vashti comes into my mind!
She disobeyed my order at the feast,
So she is put away, and lives in exile.
How little quiet have I known since then!
Plot, plot and counter-plot, and none to comfort,
Nor to advise, as Vashti used to do.
Was it a plot that made her disobey?
I sent Prince Memucan to bring her to me:
He brought back word that she refused to come.
How if Prince Memucan were lying to me?
Misquoting what she said, to make me rage
And put her from her place beside my throne?
For since she went Prince Memucan has been
About me day and night, and grows in power.
Who are the comrades of Prince Memucan?
Meres, Adathan; but his chiefest friend
Is Haman, my most trusted councillor.
Haman, my friend, to whom I love to give
Princedoms and palaces and silver mines.
And yet, what if the two conspired together
To rid me of the Queen, that they might rule me?
I will send Memucan beyond the seas

Upon some dangerous mission of great honour:
He shall away to-morrow in all haste.
But Haman I can trust.

(*He tries to compose himself to sleep.*)

Princedoms, and palaces, and silver mines,
Pomps, glories, splendours, princedoms, palaces,—
Vashti the Queen, and enemies, and princedoms—
A long, long life, and heavy hours of time!

(*He sleeps.*)

(*A clink of metal to mark passage of time.   Strike a bell or metal
plate thrice.   Count 20 slowly.*)

AHASUERUS

(*Starting up.*)

It was not I,
It was the slave Harbonah poisoned him,
Not I. I was not there. I never knew.
Horrible white face with the blotch of death;
Harbonah gave it in the honey cake—
The honey cake, I never gave it you.
I was not at the feast, it is well known
I was most sick that night.

(*He wakes.*)

Merach! Merach! begone! It was not Merach,
But someone at the footing of the bed.
Someone, a Jew, with bones instead of face
And blood that dripped.

(*He gropes at foot of bed.*)

(*He rises.*)

O blessed night, so full of peace, so calm,
After that horror.
              Ah! I know it now,
What the Chaldean told me long ago,
That I should know no quiet rest at night,

Being a King, unless I ate of bread
Baked in a house where sorrow never came.
O blessed bread, would I could eat of thee!

(Goes Back.)

Guards! are the gates secure?

GUARD

(Off.)

God save the King!
The King's gates are made sure, and the gates' keys
Here, under guard.   May the King live for ever!
(AHASUERUS *comes down Centre, then half-way back to* GUARD.)

AHASUERUS

The sentries on the walls; do they report
All quiet in the city?

GUARD

All, great King.

AHASUERUS

No armed men moving, no suspicious thing?

GUARD

Nothing, O Son of Heaven, but silent darkness,
And here and there a priest of the great sun
Praying long life and blessing on our Monarch.

AHASUERUS

(Coming down.)

Long life, long misery!

(Count 10 slowly.)

It is within this room the horror is—
That thing, that Jew, that thing out of the grave.

No, nothing, nothing! I can see there's nothing.
So—I will sleep. I will repeat that song

Made long ago by one who could not sleep,
To help his fellow-sufferers.

(Repeats.)

Along the beach a wave comes slowly in,
   And breaks, and dies away, and dies away;
      The moon is dimmed and all the ropes are taut.
Along the beach a wave comes slowly in,
   And breaks and dies away, and dies away.
      It is no season, sailor, to quit port.
Along—etc.

He sleeps.)

(<i>Count 10 slowly.   Enter</i> GHOST OF THARES, <i>Right.   The</i> GHOST
    comes behind AHASUERUS and across stage to Left Centre.   It
    stands still and hinnies like a snipe.</i>)

AHASUERUS
(In his sleep.)

O no! Spare me! Spare me!
Loose me my hands. O they have tied my feet!
I cannot get from bed, and now they come.
Merciful Gods! my thigh-bones are both broken.
I cannot stir. Who is it gibbering there?
The blood is on the bed-clothes wetting me.
Who are you? Who?

THARES
(In a disguised, piping voice.)

The shadow of what I was.
Come for your blood.

AHASUERUS

    I'll give you gold—my kingdom—
But let me go!

THARES
(Creeping slowly across, hands out.)

I cannot, Ahasuerus.

I want your life, the soul out of your body.
See, I come nearer and a little nearer,
A little nearer still, and put out hands—
Lean, skinny hands, that used to serve your food,
Thin hands to put your powerless hands aside
And take you by the throat as now I do,
And squeeze, and squeeze the life out of your flesh!

(*He begins to strangle* AHASUERUS.)

AHASUERUS

(*With effort.*)

Ah, gods! He kills me! Kills me!
Out, O gods!
            Hydaspes! Help!
Hydaspes! Guards! Hydaspes!

(*Exit* THARES, *L.*)

HYDASPES

(*R.*)
Lord!

AHASUERUS

The villain strangled me. It was a dream.
A dreadful dream! And yet I knew his face.
Who was the man? One who made plots against me,
And died, from torture, as a due reward.
Who was the man?
            Go, bring the records here,
The wise Chaldeans and the record-writers,
And let them read the records, for I know
The man's name will be there.

(*Exit* HYDASPES, *Left.*)
            It was his spirit.
An evil thing, a harbinger of evil,
A plotter coming as the vulture comes

Before the corpse.   But the Chaldean scribes
Will know his name, and by their magicry
Tell me what evil comes.

                    Thares it was—
Thares, the man was, who was put to death
For plotting with the other, Bigdana.

                                        (Goes Back.)

Let pass the wise Chaldeans when they come.

                    THE GUARD

                                        (Off.)

God save the King!   May the King live for ever!

                    CURTAIN

ACT III

SCENE:—*The Throne Room of* AHASUERUS.   *Throne Settle.*
      (HYDASPES *discovered.*   HAMAN *enters Left.*)

                    HAMAN

Why do you bring me to this fearful place
Even before the dawn?

                    HYDASPES

                    You trust to me:
Anywhere else we might be overheard.

                    HAMAN

What is the secret that you wish to tell me?

                    HYDASPES

Lord, I know well that I have sworn to you
To tell you all the secrets of the palace.

The King is overwhelmed in utter gloom.
During this night a ghastly dream has scared him;
In the calm silence of the night he shrieked;
I hurried in; I found him babbling wildly,
Talking of peril threatening him with death,
Of enemies, of evil, and of Esther.
And in these horrors did he pass the night;
Then, weary from the sleep which fled from him,
He tried to clear his spirit of the horror
And bade men bring him in the written records,
Telling of all his glory, and his reign.
There in his bed he rests while these are read.

HAMAN

What portion of his reign is being read?

HYDASPES

All of his glorious time since he was King.

HAMAN

Has he forgotten now his ghastly dream?

HYDASPES

He has assembled all his great magicians
Who read the will of Heaven in darksome dreams.
But you yourself seem troubled as by dreams;
You seem dismayed: have you some secret trouble?

(HAMAN *turns.*)

HAMAN

Can you ask that, and see my situation?
Hated, feared, envied by the men I crush.

(*Folds arms.*)

HYDASPES

Ah, upon whom has Heaven smiled more gently?
You see the whole world prostrate at your feet.

HAMAN

The whole world? Every day a filthy slave,
With brazen brow, disdains and injures me.

HYDASPES

Who is this enemy of State and King?

HAMAN

You know, perhaps, the name of Mordecai?

HYDASPES

Chief of an impious and rebellious race?

HAMAN

Yes, he.

HYDASPES

Lord, can so weak a foeman trouble you?

HAMAN

The insolent scoundrel never bows to me.
When all the Persians bow with holy awe
And dare not raise their foreheads from the earth,
He, proudly seated, with unbended head,
Treats all my honour as impiety
And looks at me with a seditious brow;
And day and night he haunts the palace door.
Always, when I go out or enter in,
His hateful face afflicts me and pursues me,
And all night long my troubled spirit sees him.

(Right down stage.)

This morning I, though up before the dawn,
Found him before me, smeared with filthy dust,
Dressed all in rags, all pale; but still his eye
Kept underneath the ashes the same pride.
Dear friend, how does he dare this brazen boldness?
You, who see all that passes in the palace,

Do you believe that friends encourage him?
What backing has he?

HYDASPES

My Lord, you know that it was he discovered
That bloody plot of Thares to the King.
The King then promised to reward him well,
Though since that time he has forgotten it.

HAMAN

I as a young child came among the Persians;
I govern now where I was made a slave;
My wealth is equal to the wealth of kings,
Only my forehead wants the royal crown.

(*Crosses to Right in front of* HYDASPES.)

Yet all my honour is but little to me
While Mordecai at the palace entrance
Tortures my spirit with a thousand daggers,
And all my grandeur seems to me as none
While that vile slave is lighted by the sun.

HYDASPES

(*Moves down to Left.*)

You will be rid of him in ten hours' time;
The whole Jew race is promised to the vultures.

HAMAN

Ah! 'tis a long, long time to my impatience.

(*Sits on throne.*)

Listen, I'll tell the story of my vengeance.
It was through him, who would not bow to me,
That I have caused this sentence that destroys them—
Vengeance too little for a man so foul.
For when one dares affront a man like Haman,
The following vengeance cannot be too great.
One must have vengeance

Such as will make the universe to tremble,
So that the whole Jew race be drowned in blood.
I wish that some day in the startled centuries
A man shall say: "Yes, once there were the Jews,
An insolent race that covered all the world;
But one of them dares stir the wrath of Haman:
Immediately they disappeared from earth."

HYDASPES

Lord, is it your Amalekitish blood
That secretly excites you to destroy them?

HAMAN

I know the bloody feud there was of old
Between the Jews and the Amalekites;
But I am so attached to worldly greatness,
I do not feel this racial prejudice.
Mordecai is guilty, that suffices;
And so I stirred Ahasuerus' mind;

(Change of voice to venom.)

I told him lies, invented calumnies,
Touched him with fear, and left him terrified;
Told him the Jews were arming,
Rich, seditious,
Their very God hateful to other gods.
I told the King "These strangers only hope
To wreck the peace in which we find ourselves.
Strike them," I said, "before they strike at you
And fill your treasure-houses with their booty."
I told him, he believed me, and at once
The King gave me the seal of Royal Power.
"Save me," he said, "protect our royal peace,
Ruin those scoundrels and their wealth is yours."
All of the Jewish race was thus condemned,
I and the King arranged the day of slaughter.

But to await ten hours that traitor's death
Is too much anguish to my aching heart.
Something, I know not what poisons my joy:
Why must I see that scoundrel ten hours more?

HYDASPES

Can you not have him killed with but one word?
Lord, ask the King to give him up to you.

HAMAN

That's why I am here, seeking a fitting moment.
You know as well as I this pitiless Prince,
How terrible his sudden rage can be;
Often he breaks the network of our plans.

(*Pause.*)

My fear too subtly works to torture me;
The Jew to him must be too vile a soul.

HYDASPES

O why delay? Go, build the gallows for him.

HAMAN

There's noise—I go. If the King calls for me—

HYDASPES

Enough.

(*They go off Left to wings.*)
(*Enter* AHASUERUS *and* ASAPH.)

AHASUERUS

So then, without this faithful information,
Two traitors would have killed their King in bed.
Let people leave me;

(*Exit of* HYDASPES *and* HAMAN.)

Asaph, stay with me.

(ASAPH *behind* KING. KING *sits on throne.*)

I must confess I had forgotten them,
Almost forgotten their most bloody crime;
And now this reading brings it back to me,
I see again the end their crime achieved
And how by torments they were put to death.
Now, of that faithful subject, whose quick eye
Unravelled all the thread of their black plot
Through whom, in fact, Persia and I were saved,
What honour, what rewards were given to him?

ASAPH

They promised much, and that is all I know.

AHASUERUS

Wicked forgetfulness of such great service,
Certain effect of my too busy life.
A Prince is ever weighed with busy cares,
Dragged on unendingly from thing to thing;
The future troubles him, the present strikes him,
But swifter than the light the past escapes him.
Ah, rather let the crime escape by vengeance
Than such rare service lose its right reward.
That man who showed such noble zeal for me—
Is he alive?

ASAPH

He sees the star that lights you.

AHASUERUS

Why has he not demanded his reward?
What distant country hides him from my love?

ASAPH

Lord, uncomplaining of yourself and fate,
He drags his life out at your palace doors.

AHASUERUS

What is his name?

ASAPH

His name is Mordecai.

AHASUERUS

What is his country?

ASAPH

Lord, since I have to tell you,
He is a captive Jew, condemned to death.

AHASUERUS

He is a Jew? O Heaven, when my life
Was threatened to be taken by my subjects,
A Jew protects me from my subjects' swords;
A Jew has saved me from the Persians' vengeance!
But since he saved me, be he what he may—
Here! someone!   (*Calls*.)
                            (*Enter* HYDASPES, *Left*.)

HYDASPES

Lord?

AHASUERUS

Look by that door,
See if some noble of my Court is there.

HYDASPES

Haman is at your door, since before dawn.

AHASUERUS

Let him come in, he may enlighten me.

                    (HYDASPES *bows and exit*.)
                        (*Enter* HAMAN, *Left*.)

Hail, happy standfast of thy master's throne,
Soul of my counsel, who so many times
Has lightened in my hand my heavy sceptre.
A dark reproach embarrasses my soul.

I know how pure a zeal inflames your heart,
I know no lying ever stains your lips,
I know my interest only is your thought,
So tell me,
      What ought a very mighty prince to do
To honour any subject whom he loves?
By what great glory worthy of a King
Can I reward a man of faith and merit?
Put not a limit on my condescension,
Think of my power ere you answer me.

HAMAN

(Aside.)

Haman, it is for you yourself you speak;
      (Comes down stage and speaks to audience.)
What other subject could he wish to honour?

AHASUERUS

What do you think?

HAMAN

O King, I think of all the Persian Kings,
Remembering what they did on such occasions
But bring them back in vain into my mind.

*(He begins to move back, so that five lines from this he is slightly
    behind* AHASUERUS.)

How should their deeds make precedents for you?
For what are they when put beside yourself?
Your reign will serve as model to all time.
You wish then to reward some faithful subject?
Honour alone rewards a noble mind.

     *(*HAMAN *gets behind to Left of* AHASUERUS.)

Lord, I should wish that he, that happy mortal,
Should like yourself, be decked to-day in purple,
And wear a sacred crown upon his brow,
And go through Shushan with the world to see,

Riding upon your war-horse gloriously.
And as a crown to this magnificence,
(*During these lines he comes forward down stage, and, though
speaking to* AHASUERUS, *is carried away by his own elo-
quence.*)
Let some great Lord, magnificent in power,
The next man in the Empire to yourself,
Lead the proud war-horse by the bridle rein;
And let the proud Lord in his courtly dress,
Cry with a high voice in the public places:
"Mortals, prostrate yourselves, 'tis thus the King
Crowns faith and honours merit."

(*Pause.*)

AHASUERUS

I see that wisdom's self inspires you,
In every point your judgment backs my will.
Go, lose no time; what you have said to me
I wish in every point to be made good.
Virtue no longer shall be hidden here.
Go then, O Haman, to the palace gates.

(*Pause.* HAMAN *shows joy.*)

There you will find the poor Jew Mordecai—

(*Pause.* HAMAN *shows more joy.*)

He is the man whom I desire to honour.
Order his triumph, march before him, you;
Let your voice ring through Shushan with his name,
Let every knee bend wheresoe'er he comes.
Now leave me, all.

HAMAN

(*Aside.*)

Gods!

(*Exit* HAMAN.)

AHASUERUS.

Never has subject gloried in such honour,

But yet I show how deeply I can fear
To be ungrateful;
                            And the world will see
The innocent distinguished from the guilty.
Yet all the same, that loathsome race of Jews—

(ESTHER, RACHEL *and* CHORUS *enter Left, crouching.*)

What insolent mortal comes to look for death,
Entering without my orders?
Guards! Guards! What, Esther, you?
You here and unexpected!

ESTHER

(*Swooning.*)

O children, hold your Queen!

(RACHEL *on* ESTHER'S *left, and* 1ST *and* 2ND CHORUS *support her.*)

I die!

AHASUERUS

No, Esther, what do you fear?
                            No; do not think
I made this bitter order against you.
Live, for you see I stretch my golden sceptre
Towards you, as a witness of my pardon.

ESTHER

What friendly voice commands that I should live?

AHASUERUS

Do you not recognize your husband's voice?

ESTHER

Lord, I have never witnessed save with fear
The majesty upon your kingly brow;
Judge then the terror in my troubled soul
To see that brow in anger against me.

What daring heart could see without a shudder,
Or bear the light that glitters from your eyes
Like the bright anger of the Living God!

AHASUERUS

O sun! O fires of immortal light—
I too am troubled and can hardly bear
To see, as now, her terror and dismay.
O Queen, put by the terror that o'erwhelms you,
You are the mistress of my kingly heart.
Come, test my friendship for you. What you will—
What will you have? The half of my possessions?

ESTHER

And can a King, obeyed by the whole world,

(*Kneeling.*)

Before whom all must bow and kiss the dust,
Look with such kindness on his meanest slave?

AHASUERUS

This sceptre, and this Empire, and this terror,
And these profound respects, and all this pomp,
Bring little sweetness to me and fatigue me,
Believe me, Esther. But I find in you
A grace that charms me and that never tires,
Nothing but innocence, and peace, and beauty,
That drives the darkness of my troubles from me
And makes less fearful all the rage of foes.
Therefore, without this terror, answer me:
Tell me what thrilling business brings you here,
What care, what trouble, makes you shudder thus?
Speak; you have but to ask, to have your will,
If aught you wish is in a mortal's giving.

ESTHER

O goodness of my King!
Indeed a thrilling business brings me here.

Here I await my happiness or death;
All, mighty King, depends upon your will;
One word from you may end my agony
And make me happiest of the queens on earth.

AHASUERUS

Speak! You inflame my wish to hear your trouble.

ESTHER

Lord, if I found a favour in your eyes,

(*On her knees.*)

If ever you consented to my prayers,
Grant before all that I this day receive you,
My lord and sovereign, at a solemn feast,
And grant that Haman be invited thither;
For before him I'll dare to break my silence
And also tell why I demand his presence.

(CHORUS *stand.*)

AHASUERUS

Esther, you trouble me; yet be it so.
Let all be done as you desire it.

(*Order to* GUARD.)

You!—Seek for Haman; let him understand
He is invited by the Queen to feast.

(*Exit* GUARD, *Left.*)
(*Enter* HYDASPES, *Right. Comes down below* KING.)

HYDASPES

The wise Chaldeans are assembled here,
According to your order.

AHASUERUS

Princess, a strange dream occupies my thought;
The answer of the wise men affects you.
Come! you shall hear them from behind a curtain,
And afterwards shall give me your advice.

I fear some treacherous enemy plots against us.
Follow me, Esther.

ESTHER

You, my gentle friends,
Wait here till I return.

(AHASUERUS *and* ESTHER *go off, Right.*)

(RACHEL *crosses Right, then turns and speaks. As she speaks*
the CHORUS *come down the stage.*)

RACHEL

What do you think, my sisters, of our fortunes?
Which do you think will triumph,
Esther or Haman?
Will God's will, or will man's will triumph here?

1ST CHORUS

We cannot tell. We know that God's great Hand
Is heavy on the race of Jews this day.

2ND CHORUS

It is because of sin, because of blood,
   Blood of just men, shed in iniquity,
That we, the lost, are trampled to the mud
   And are condemned to die in slavery.

Soon, when the evening comes, our foes will seek
   All of our race. Their bloody swords will slay
Men, women, children, all, the strong and weak,
   And heap our mangled bodies by the way,
      To know no burial.

(Kneel here.)

Lord, if we search our ways and turn again,
   Surely Thou wilt forgive, and Thou wilt send
Help, like an army, mercy like the rain,
   And save us from destruction at the end.
      Save us, O save us!

The doom is cast, our murderers draw the sword,
None can avert our death but Thou, O Lord!

Without, our murderers hasten even now.
We are as dead, and none can save but Thou.

CURTAIN

ACT IV

In Front of Curtain, on a platform or avant-scène, (HAMAN,
ZERESH.)

ZERESH

Here, by the still shut gate of Esther's hall,
Hark to your wife; by all that you hold sacred,
My Lord, hide your blind rage against the Jews,
Make bright that forehead shadowed now with sadness:
Kings fear reproach, and sadness
You, chosen by the Queen, the one guest asked,
Show that you feel that proud felicity,
Show that you feel it, even through any evil.
I have a hundred times been told by you
That he who cannot stomach an affront
Nor hide his proper feelings with false colours,
Should fly from Courts and Kings.
All men have disappointments: often, too,
An outrage bravely borne, endured with prudence,
Has led a man even to the highest honours.

HAMAN

Misery! misery, frightful to my thought!
O shame that never can be wiped away!
A loathsome Jew, the foulest of his kind,
Has now been clad in purple by these hands.

It's not enough that he should conquer me,
That I have served as herald to his glory,
While he, the traitor, mocked at my confusion;
And all the people mocking after him,
Seeing the blushes covering my face,
Mocked me and muttered of my certain fall.
O cruel King! And this has been your pleasure!
You only gave me honours in the past
To make me feel your tyranny the better
And drive me deeper still in ignominy.

ZERESH

Why judge so harshly of the King's intention?
He thinks that he rewards a generous deed.
Ought one not rather to be much astonished
That he so long has left it unrewarded?
He has done nothing but by your advice,
And you yourself dictated all the ceremony.
In all the Empire you are next to him;
Say, does he know how much you loathe the Jew?

HAMAN

The King knows well how much he owes to me;
The King knows well how I, to make him great,
Have stamped remorse, fear, shame, beneath my feet,
And used his power with a heart of brass,
Silenced the laws, made innocent people sob,
Only for him contemned the Persians' hatred,
Cherished and sought the curses of the people.
And for reward, the barbarous King to-day
Exposed me to their mocking and their hatred.

ZERESH

My Lord, let me speak plain. That zeal you show,
That zeal of bending all things to his power,
Had it a purer object than yourself?

Take without going further this one case:
Of all the ruined Jews made desolate,
Surely you ruined them to please yourself!
Can you not rightly fear that even now
The people loathe us, and the Court detests us?

(HAMAN *turns away*.)

Lord, I *must* speak. My Lord, this Jew—this Jew
Heaped now with honours, frightens me.
Misfortunes often follow on each other,
The Jewish race always brought death to yours.
Take now this morning's trouble as an omen:
Perhaps your fortune is about to leave you;
Fortune is fickle. Act before she leaves you.

(*She touches him.*)

My lord, what more ambition can you have?
I shudder when I see the way you take.

(*He turns slightly to her. He is below her.*)

The deep abysses opening before me.
Nought but a horrible fall before our feet.
Lord, let us fly,

(*Here she holds him by the shoulder.*)

And seek some calmer fate,
Fly to the Hellespont and those far shores
Where in old time your wandering fathers were.
Let us away, away from fortune's malice!
Send on our richest treasures ere we start;
Leave me to manage: I will take the children,—
Have no more care except to hide yourself,
For the most terrible and stormy sea
Is safer to us than this treacherous Court.
But someone hurriedly is coming here!

(*Enter* HYDASPES *from below, in front, Left.*)

HYDASPES

My Lord, I came to seek you:
Your absence takes away the general joy,
Ahasuerus bids me bring you to him.

HAMAN

Is Mordecai also at this feast?

HYDASPES

Why do you let this image of the Jew
Torment you even as a royal guest?
Let the Jew glory in his petty triumph,
Can he avoid the fury of the King?
You rule Ahasuerus heart and soul;
The Jew has been rewarded, but next time
Will be beheaded.
We have but garlanded your victim for you.
And I suspect that you, when backed by Esther,
Will come to even greater honours here.

HAMAN

O could I but believe your joyful news!

HYDASPES

I heard the answers of the wise Chaldeans.
They say a treacherous stranger plots and plans
To kill the Queen.
The King, who does not know this guilty traitor,
Thinks that the plan is plotted by the Jews.

HAMAN

Dear friend, the Jews are truly but wild beasts;
One must above all fear their daring Chief.
Earth has too long endured the horror of them,
Nature cannot be too soon rid of them.
So now I breathe again.
            Good-bye, dear Zeresh!

HYDASPES

Enter, receive the honour ready for you.

(*Curtain rises and discovers* AHASUERUS, ESTHER. HAMAN *entering.*)

AHASUERUS.

(*To* ESTHER *at his right.*)

Ah! Your last speeches have a secret grace;
All that you do displays a noble mind
Beyond all price, beyond all gold or purple.
What virtuous country bore so rare a treasure?
What wisdom reared you in your infancy?
But tell me what it is you want from me,
For all your wishes, Esther, shall be granted,
Even to the half of this my powerful Empire.
This that I promised once, I now repeat.

ESTHER

No such great wishes, Lord: but this I long for,
Since even my King himself has bid me speak.

(*She flings herself at his feet.*)

I dare beseech you both for my own life
And the salvation of a wretched people
That you have now condemned to die with me.

AHASUERUS

(*Raising her.*)

To die? And you?
            What people? What is this?

HAMAN

(*Aside.*)

I tremble!

ESTHER

Esther, my Lord, her father was a Jew.
You know the harshness of your cruel orders.

Haman

(*Aside.*)

Ah, gods!

Ahasuerus

Ah! what a blow! you pierce me to the heart.
You, daughter of a Jew?
                              You whom I love!
Goodness and innocence their very selves!
Esther, whom I believed did come from Heaven,
Is after all born from this impure stock!
Unhappy King!

Esther

                              You can reject my prayer,
But I demand at least for a last grace
That you should hear me speak, Lord, to the end,
And above all, let Haman check me not.

Ahasuerus

Speak!

Esther

    O God, confound daring and knavery!
These Jews of whom you mean to rid the world,
Whom you believe the outcasts of mankind,
Were sovereigns in a happy land of old
While they were faithful to their fathers' God:
God, only Master of the earth and skies,
The Eternal One, the Maker of the world,
Who hears the sighing of the tortured poor.
There came a day the Jews neglected Him,
They dared raise altars unto other gods,
And in a day kings, peoples, all were scattered,
And their Assyrian captivity
Became the just reward of their unfaith.
The time went by, and after many years

The captive Jews enjoyed a happier lot.
You became King, you, friend of innocence,
Whose mercy all declared with cries of joy.
But cruel minds surround the gentlest princes
And poison even the gentlest mind with lies;
And here a ruffian from the depths of Thrace
Comes to encourage cruelty in you;
A statesman, hating you and all your glory.

HAMAN

Your glory? I? Can you believe it, Heaven?
I, with no other aim, no other god!

AHASUERUS

Silence!

Do you dare speak before the King commands?

ESTHER

You see our cruel enemy before you;
'Tis he, this faithless and barbarian statesman,
Who with malignant zeal blinding your eyes,
Has armed your strength against our innocence.
Who but a pitiless Scythian would have dared
Dictate an order of such frightful horror
And give a signal through the startled world
To fill the globe with murders?
                              Who but he?
Under your name, most just of Emperors,
This faithless stranger desolates your country;
Even in this palace will his bloody rage
Spill your good subjects' blood.
What have the Jews done to provoke his hate?
What civil quarrel have we helped to spread?
When have the Jews marched with your enemies?
Were ever slaves more passive to the yoke,

Worshipping in their chains the God Who gives them.
Lord, while your hand lay heaviest upon them,
They prayed their God to be a guard to you,
To break the plots the wicked made against you
And take your throne in the shadow of His wings.
And doubt not, Lord, God was your help and stay,
Beat down the Parthians and the Indians for you,
Scattered before you all the Scythian hordes
And to the eyes of one poor Jew discovered
The plans of men who plotted to destroy you.
I am that same poor Jew's adopted daughter.

AHASUERUS

Mordecai?

ESTHER

He was the sole survivor of our household.
My father was his brother. He, like me,
Is in direct descent from our first King.
Full of just horror for an Amalekite,
A race accursed by the lips of God,
He would not bow the knee to Haman here,
Nor give him honours only due to you.
From this, my Lord, hidden under other names,
Proceeds his hatred against all the Jews.
In vain you gave rewards to Mordecai,
Already at the very door of Haman
Behold the gallows Haman has prepared!
Within this hour, that reverend old man,
Dragged from your palace precincts by his order,
Dressed in your kingly purple, will be hanged.

AHASUERUS

What light, what horror burst upon my soul!

(Rising.)

My blood is all aflame with shame and rage.
I was his plaything, then! Heaven lighten me!

One moment—let me think.
Call Mordecai. I will hear his statement.

(*Exit* AHASUERUS.)

HAMAN

(*To* ESTHER.)

Queen, I am stricken with amazement here.
I am deceived; nay, I have been betrayed
By those that hate the Jews, heaven be my witness.
By slaying them I thought to save yourself,
Use all my credit, Queen, on their behalf,
You see the King is staggered by the news.
I know how one can press or check the King;
I make him calm or raging as I please.
The interests of the Jews are sacred to me.
Speak, Queen, I swear and your dead enemies
Shall make amends if I have injured you.
Whom would you have destroyed?

ESTHER

Go, traitor! leave me.
Jews expect nothing from a wretch like you.
O miserable man! Avenging God,
Ready to judge you, holds His balance up.
Soon shall just sentence be pronounced on you.
Tremble! God's reign approaches, thine is over.

HAMAN

Yes, I confess thy God a fearful God;
But will He cherish pitiless hate against me?
Ah! it is done, my pride is forced to bend,
Pitiless Haman is reduced to prayer!

(*Flings himself at* ESTHER'S *feet*. ESTHER *moves to the centre.*)

By the salvation of the Jews, O Queen,
And by these queenly feet that I embrace,

And by that wise old man, your kingdom's honour,
Deign to appease the rage of this fierce King;
Save Haman, trembling at your sacred knees!

(Enter AHASUERUS.)

AHASUERUS

This traitor dares to put his hands upon you!

(HAMAN up.)

I read his treachery in his guilty eyes,
His guilty looks confirm what you have said
And show me all the course of his attempt.
Tear the dog's spirit out this very instant
Before his door, instead of Mordecai,
And let his death appease the earth and skies.
Then let his body be a public show.

(HAMAN led away by GUARDS.)
(Enter MORDECAI in front.)

Man loved of Heaven, my safety and my joy,
Thy King is no more governed by the wicked;
My eyes have seen the truth.   Crime is confounded.
Come, shine beside me,

(MORDECAI is led to the QUEEN'S seat, right of AHASUERUS.)

Ranked as is your due,

Prince of my realm and chiefest Counsellor.
I have been blind; but now, no longer blind,
I put my trust in one whom age makes wise,
And wisdom merciful, and mercy blessed.
By God's great sun your lightest word this day
Shall be a law to Persia for all time.

MORDECAI

O King, whom Heaven ever keep in care,
The peril presses on the Jews.

Lord, save them!

AHASUERUS

They shall be saved.   Come take these orders out;
Revoke the cruel edict of that man.

(A Guard takes orders.)

CHORUS

Bountiful mercy of our guardian God,
O star in darkness, O white light of dawn,
After the night; O blessed touch of rain,
Changing the desert's salty sand to flowers;
O well of water in the blinding heat,
When even the asp goes mad; O shining city
Seen by the footsore after hours of travel;
O land, that far away, beyond wild water,
Gleams out at evening; O port of peace
After the sea; we thank Thee for this mercy.

1ST CHORUS

Once, when of old the King of Egypt followed,
With hosts of horse, our fathers as they fled,
God made the sea a road for us to tread,
Made the rock give us drink, the desert bread,
But smote our foes.   His sea rose, they were swallowed.

2ND CHORUS

And as our fathers wandered then
    God guided them to their desire
By a bright angel in the hearts of men,
    And in the day by cloud and in the night by fire.
Until they reached the green land full of springs.
The cornland that men reap but need not plough,
    The happy hill;
All the way there God hid them in His wings,
Even as He hides us now, and ever will,
    And ever will!

1st Chorus

Though men deal proudly, God is over them.

(*A crying without.*)

Ahasuerus

What is the noise of tumult in the street?

Chorus

Sounds as of slaying and of lamentation.

Esther

O King, I dread that crying in the city!
It must be that your orders come too late
To save our fellow-captives.   Swords are flashing,
And there are screams of women, and men falling.
Hark, King, they kill the Jews!

Chorus

O Heaven, save them!

Save us, O Heaven!

Ahasuerus

By the fires of Bel

I am too late!

(*Enter* Asaph, *Left.*)

What is it, Asaph?   Speak!

Asaph

O King, my spirit faints, I cannot speak.

Ahasuerus

Is murder being done without there?

Asaph

Yes.

Or no, not murder, but a red accounting,
A settling for old sin.   Unseen by us,
Unseen in the air about us, our bad deeds

Grow into devils, who in our happy time,
When it is sunshine with us, startle out
And take us by the throat and shatter us.

AHASUERUS

Are you so taken by the throat? You shudder
Like one with the fever, and your lips are white.

ASAPH

O King, I shudder at the risk you ran.

AHASUERUS

The Queen ran risk, not I.

ASAPH

                    No. Hark, my Lord.
When you did bid us take that traitor hence,
We dragged him out, and down the corridor
Past the bronze doorways of Prince Memucan.
There, with full voice, he shouted: "Memucan,
Meres, Adathan, help me! Call our friends!
All is discovered! Save me! Kill the King!
Rush in and kill him! Save me! Memucan,
You swore to kill him. I am to be killed.
Memucan's men, come, save me! Kill these dogs,
And kill the King! You shall have all my wealth,
My silver mines, my palaces, all, all,
And be my princes."
                    But he called in vain.
Prince Memucan was gone, with all his men,
Gone over sea this morning at your bidding.
He called to empty courts where doves picked food
And the pale fountain trembled like an aspen.
Then, seeing that none answered, he was stilled.
A shuddering took him, and he called for drink,
And prayed that he might be brought back to you,
To tell you all the plot of Memucan,

That you might spare his life.
I, having my orders, told him he must die.
By this time we had reached his palace gate
And stood beneath the gallows he had built.
There, where he planned to murder Mordecai,
Men put a rope about his own doomed neck.
Then he besought a grace, he asked the time.
We told him, "Almost the fifth hour;" and he
Smiled haggardly and said, "Astrologers
Foretold that on this day at the fifth hour
A great event would alter life for me.
Wait till the hour, one little minute's peace,
While I pray God."
              We waited, while he prayed.
And the square filled with silent men and women,
His victims, now avenged.
They were as silent as a forest is
In the great heat before a thunderstorm,
Before the first few drops strike the parched leaves.
But one mad woman, who had lost her son,
Babbled, "He will escape, for all their power!"
It wanted but a minute of the hour
Of Fifth Hour Sacrifice. The ankle bells
Tinkled as women passed; the old priests shuffled,
Lighting the incense in the temple braziers,
And acolytes in red came to the gates.
O King, I shudder at that ruffian's guile.
Even as the trumpet of the hour sounded,
There came the clink of arms, and swordsmen came
(A band of swordsmen, Prince Adathan's men)
Up from the water gateway to the square.
Then Haman shouted, "Help, Adathan's men!
Adathan, help! See! I am Haman here.
Charge! Set upon these guards and set me free."
Then with a cheer those swordsmen charged the gallows

And bore us back, and snatched him from our hands.
But at that word of setting Haman free
Those silent watchers there, the multitude,
His victims from of old, the men ground down,
The women bartered and the children stunted,
Screamed all together in a venomous hate,
And seizing stones and sticks, or with bare hands,
They set upon those swordsmen of Adathan's
And routed them; so we recovered Haman.
            And Haman bit his lips
And said: "Those were the swordsmen I had hired
To kill the Jews indeed, but afterward
To kill the King and crown me King instead.
I should have been a King at this Fifth Hour.
Only have mercy, I will tell you all."
Lord, I have looked on fire and on flood,
Both are less terrible than the mob in rage.
When he cried "Mercy," all that sea of men
Roared like a battle, rose like a toppling tide,
Swept over him and choked him out of life.
The Jews are saved: Haman is dead. The crowd
Tore him piecemeal. Now, by the rope that choked him,
They drag his corpse to be a public show.
This is the seal of office that he held.

                                    (*Gives signet.*)

AHASUERUS

Prince Mordecai, take this seal of office.
I give you Haman's property and power;
Possess in justice his ill-gotten wealth.
I break the fatal slavery of the Jews.
All who elect to stay in Persia here
Are henceforth equal with my Persian subjects;
All who would fain go home, are free to go.
And, so that men may tremble at the Name
Of Esther's God, I will rebuild His Temple,

Using sweet cedar where the Jews put oak,
Marble instead of stone, and gold for brass.
And may the Jews in all their solemn feasts
Keep this day's triumph holy, and my name
Forever living in their memory.

ESTHER

O God, by roads unknown to mortal men
Thy wisdom brings eternal plans to be!

CHORUS

Even but now our enemies beset our feet to ruin us;
But in the darkness of our doom there rose a star to lighten us!

The proud man planned to shed our blood; his voice went
    ringing to the sky;
His sin has turned upon himself; his bloody thoughts have
    made him die.

Now like a cedar that the storm uproots on windy Lebanon,
He lies on earth: I passed his haunt, but God had blown and
    he was gone.

                    (*Here the* KING *and* ESTHER *move off Right.*)
(*The* CHORUS *come slowly down stage speaking, and pass off in
    front.*)

Esther has saved us: we are raised out of the dust: we are set
    free;
We may go home to Zion's hill, forgetting all our slavery.

We may rebuild the sacred town and tread the dear green fields
    again;
We are set free to love and live, forgetting all these years of
    pain.

Let us give thanks that pride has fall'n. The evils that the
 wicked shape
Come by one road, but God has made a myriad pathways of
 escape.

(They leave the stage here.)

And when the evil presses worst, seeming to triumph over good,
There comes, as here, the thing that saves, by secret ways not
 understood.

(They pass away.)

CURTAIN

BERENICE

A TRAGEDY BY RACINE

BERENICE

PERSONS

TITUS
BERENICE
ANTIOCHUS
PAULINUS
ARSACES
PHENICE
RUTILIUS

BERENICE

ACT I

ANTIOCHUS

Let us stay here a moment. I can see
That all this stately palace is unknown
To you, Arsaces.
This lonely room is where the Emperor comes
To find some quiet from the cares of Court.
Here sometimes, too, he comes to see the Queen:
The Queen's apartments lie beyond that door.
And now, Arsaces, go to see the Queen,
And tell her that I beg that she will grant
What I dare ask, some secret words with me.
Say I regret to be importunate.

ARSACES

You, Lord, importunate? You, her faithful friend;
You, generously careful of her interests;
You, that Antiochus who loved her once,
One of the greatest Kings in all the East!
Even if she be about to marry Titus,
Does that put such a distance 'twixt you two?

ANTIOCHUS

No. Go, my friend. Mind not those other matters;
See if I may but speak with her alone.

(*Exit* ARSACES.)

Alas, Antiochus! Can I ever dare
To tell the Queen I love her? Why, I tremble
Already, and my agitated heart
Now fears the moment it so much desired.

159

Queen Berenice has left me without hope;
She ordered me never to speak of love.
Five years I have been silent, five long years,
Hiding my love under a veil of friendship.
And now to-day I have to speak with her.
Titus, they say, is marrying her to-day.
But can I think that she whom Titus plans
To make his Empress, will be kind to me
More than she was of old in Palestine?
Titus is marrying her, and at the altar
I come to tell her that I love her too.
What good can come to me from telling her?
Ah! I must go and not displease her thus.
I will withdraw, and go, and without speaking
Pass far away from her—forget her—die.

                                        (*Pause.*)

I cannot always suffer from such torment,
Nor shed these secret tears unknown to her
And lose her, through the fearing her displeasure.
Oh, lovely Queen, and why should you be vexed?
I do not come to beg you not to marry;
I do not come to beg that you should love me,
Ah! woe is me! I only come to say
That now, even now,
After so long being certain that my rival
Would find some fatal drawback to his marriage,
I find that I was wrong; that all can be,
And that your marriage now is being prepared.
Oh, sad example of long constancy!
After five years of love and empty hope
I am still faithful, though I hope no longer.
She could not blame me, she will pity me.
Whatever happens I will speak to her.
Alas! what can a hopeless lover fear,
Having resolved to see her face no more?

Can I go in, Arsaces?

ARSACES

Lord, I have seen the Queen—
I only pierced the crowd with difficulty;
She is surrounded with adoring people
Drawn to her palace by her coming greatness.
Titus has ceased his mourning for his father
And takes to wooing, and the rumour goes
That before night the happy Berenice
Will change the title "Queen" for that of "Empress."

ANTIOCHUS

Alas!

ARSACES

But how can such news trouble you?

ANTIOCHUS

So, then, I cannot speak alone with her?

ARSACES

Lord, you will see her. She has been informed
That you would see her here at once alone.
She granted your desire with a look,
And doubtless waits a favourable moment
To escape the crowds of courtiers that surround her.

ANTIOCHUS

Enough. And those important orders given—
Have you fulfilled them?

ARSACES

Lord, you know my zeal.
There are some ships prepared in Ostia harbour
Ready to sail the instant you command;
But whom do you intend to send in them?

ANTIOCHUS

One can but go when I have seen the Queen.

ARSACES

Who can but go?

ANTIOCHUS

Myself.

ARSACES

You, King Antiochus?

ANTIOCHUS

Yes, when I leave this palace,
I shall leave Rome, Arsaces, and for ever.

ARSACES

I am surprised, and justly. What, great King,
After Queen Berenice has kept you here
For three long years, far from your State, in Rome;
Now, when she needs your presence at her marriage,
When her great lover, Titus, marrying her,
Prepares such glory for her!

ANTIOCHUS

Arsaces, leave this talk, it troubles me:
Let her enjoy her fortune.

ARSACES

Ah, my Lord,
Her coming glory makes the Queen forget you,
And enmity succeeds friendship betrayed?

ANTIOCHUS

Not so. I never hated the Queen less.

ARSACES

What then? Has the new Emperor grown proud

Since his accession, and been cold to you?
Does any feeling of his change of mind
Drive you to go from Rome?

ANTIOCHUS

Titus has never seemed the colder to me.
I should be wrong to make complaint.

ARSACES

Why go, then?

What fancy makes you your own enemy?
Heaven raises to the throne a Prince who loves you,
A Prince who saw you in the war seek death
Or glory, in his steps; whose princely courage,
Helped by yourself, subdued the rebel Jews.
The Prince remembers well the famous day
Which ended the long siege. Do you remember?
The enemy quiet in their triple rampart,
Watching unharmed our impotent attacks,
And you advancing with the scaling ladders,
Carrying death among them up the walls?
That was the day, the day you were near death,
The day when Titus found you almost dead,
Bleeding from many wounds, and kissed you there
As the most gallant man in the forlorn.
Now, sir, you ought to wait for your reward
For all your blood shed then. If you must go
Back to your kingdom, go not unrewarded,
Wait till Imperial Cæsar sends you back
Laden with honours as the friend of Rome.
Can nothing change your mind? You do not answer.

ANTIOCHUS

What would you have me say?
I want one moment's speech with Berenice.

ARSACES

Well, Lord?

ANTIOCHUS

Her fate will settle mine.

ARSACES

And how?

ANTIOCHUS

I wish to hear her speak about her marriage.
If she admits the rumour to be true,
If it be true that she will marry Cæsar,
If Titus makes her Empress, I shall go.

ARSACES

What makes this marriage so distasteful to you?

ANTIOCHUS

When we have gone, I'll tell you.

ARSACES

I am troubled.

ANTIOCHUS

Here is the Queen. Good-bye; do as I bade.

(*Enter* BERENICE *and* PHENICE.)

BERENICE

At last I can escape the importunity
Of all the crowds of friends whom fortune makes me.
I come from all their tedious acclamation
To find a friend who speaks out of his heart;
And I have been impatient, for I thought
You had neglected me.
I said of old that good Antiochus
Was constant in his loving care for me;
He was my friend in good or evil fortune;
And now to-day, when the gods seem to give me

Honours, which I would gladly share with him,
This same Antiochus hides from my sight
And leaves me to an unknown crowd alone.

ANTIOCHUS

Then is it true, this that the rumour says,
That marriage is to end the long, long courtship?

BERENICE

Lord, these last days have been most sorrowful;
For this long mourning that the Emperor kept,
Had kept him from me, and his love seemed changed
From those old days when he was always with me.
Now he is silent, troubled, ever weeping,
His only speeches seem like sad farewells;
So you can judge of my anxiety.

ANTIOCHUS

Now his first tenderness has come again?

BERENICE

You saw last night how his religious cares
Were backed by solemn vote, when in full house
The Senate ranked his Father with the gods?
His pious mourning now gives place to love,
To thought for her he loves. At the same time,
Not even telling me of his intention,
He called the Senate, and by proud decree
Enlarged the frontiers of my Palestine,
Joining to it Arabia and Syria.
And if I can believe the voice of friends
And his own promises so often given,
He means to crown me Queen of that expanse,
To add to all my titles that of Empress;
And he is coming here to tell me this.

ANTIOCHUS

And I come here to say good-bye for ever.

BERENICE

What are you saying? Good-bye?
And your face changes.

ANTIOCHUS

Madam, I have to go.

BERENICE

And not say why?

ANTIOCHUS

No; I must go and see her face no more.

BERENICE

Speak, Lord! What is the mystery of your going?

ANTIOCHUS

Then listen to me for the last, last time.
Lady, if in your high degree of glory
You ever think about your childhood's home,
You may remember that I saw you there
And loved you.
You may remember, too, how once your brother,
Agrippa, spoke for me, and it may be,
Perhaps, you were not vexed to hear I loved you.
Then, to my sorrow, Titus came: he saw you,
He pleased you, for of course he came before you
In all the splendour of a man who bears
The vengeances of Rome in his two hands,
Making Judæa pale.
I think that I was one of those first conquered;
And then it came to pass that your own lips
Told me to speak no more of love to you.
And yet I hoped; a long, long time I hoped,
Following like your shadow in the palace.

And then you made me promise, made me swear
Never to speak again of love to you.
But when you made me swear, my heart knew well
That I could only love you till I die.

BERENICE

You must not say this.
ANTIOCHUS
It is five years since I said anything;
And after this I shall be silent always.
And then I went with Titus to the wars,
Hoping to die, or hoping at the least
That deeds of mine might make you hear my name.
And we were at the war, Titus and I;
All that I did was far surpassed by him.
I came behind in war, even as in love.
Then, when the war and the long siege were over,
And the last pale and bloody-featured rebels
Came from their burnt-out ruins and their hunger,
He came in triumph home, and you with him.
I stayed behind, and went from place to place,
Where you had been, where I had worshipped you;
But my despair drove me to follow you,
And Titus welcomed me and brought me here.
And then I hoped—always I had some hope—
That something here might make a way for me.
But now my fate's fulfilled; your glory comes.
There will be plenty here to pray for you,
To watch your glorious crowning, without me.
I could not bring rejoicing, only tears,
So I shall go, loving you more than ever.

BERENICE

I did not think that on my marriage day
Any man's son would dare make love to me.

I will forget all that. I'll say farewell.
God knows that in the honours coming to me
I hoped that you would watch my happiness,
Because, like all the world, I honoured you,
And Titus loved you, and you admired Titus.
Your are like Titus, and a hundred times
I have been pleased to see your likeness to him.

ANTIOCHUS

Yes, that is why I go. I go too late.
Would I had gone before, and spared myself
This news of Titus and the grief it causes,
Then I should not have heard you speak his name
Nor known your love for him, but gone, and seen
No more your eyes, which see me every day
Yet cannot notice me.
Good-bye. I go. My heart's too full to speak;
I know that I shall love you till I die.
Fear not that I shall talk of my misfortune,
But if you hear that I am dead, then think
That once I was alive. Good-bye. Good-bye.

(*Exit.*)

PHENICE

Oh, how I pity him! Such faithfulness
Deserved more luck, good Lady. Don't you pity him?

BERENICE

His going so
Leaves me, I grant you, with a troubled mind.

PHENICE

I would have kept him back.

BERENICE

I keep him back?
No; rather would I lose the memory of him.
Could I encourage such a senseless love?

PHENICE

Titus has not yet spoken out his mind.
Rome looks upon you with most jealous eyes,
Lady, the rigour of the Roman laws
Makes me afraid for you.
Romans can marry none but Roman women.
Rome hates all royalty, and you are Queen.

BERENICE

Phenice, the time for terror is gone by,
And Titus loves me.   He is all-powerful.
If he but speak, the Senate will salute him
And crown his statues with the flowering laurel.
Have you not seen the splendours of to-night?
The torches, and the lamps and bonfires burning;
The Eagles of the Army standing ranked;
The crowd of Kings, the Consuls and the Senate,
All lending all their glory to my lover.
Purple and gold and laurels for his victory,
And all those eyes from every land on earth
Staring on him alone with greedy looks,
Watching that splendid port, that gentle presence.
Oh, with what awe and with what gladness too,
All of those hearts assure him of their faith!
Can one see this not thinking as I think,
That even if he had been obscurely born,
The world would still have known him as its King?
Now, while all Rome is making prayer for Titus,
And offers sacrifice for the new reign,
Let us too go and offer prayer for him.
Then I will go to him, and we shall speak
All that our full hearts hold for one another.

CURTAIN

ACT II

(Titus, Paulinus.)

Titus

Has no one seen the King of Comagena,
Or does he know that I await him here?

Paulinus

Sir, I have seen the Queen.
The King of Comagena had been with her,
But had gone out shortly before I came.
I have left word to warn him of your orders.

Titus

Enough.   What was the Queen doing?

Paulinus

Sir, she was going out
To pray the gods for your prosperity.

Titus

Too kind Princess, alas!

Paulinus

Prince, why be sad for her?
Half of the Eastern world will now be hers.
You pity her?

Titus

Paulinus, let all leave you here with me.

(*Exit* Guards.)

Alas! Rome is uncertain of my plans
And waits to know the fortunes of the Queen.
The secrets of her heart and mine, Paulinus,
Are now the talk of all the earthly world.
Now the time comes, I must explain myself.

What do they say about the Queen and me?
Speak; what do you hear?

PAULINUS

I hear on every side
About your virtue, Emperor, and her beauty.

TITUS

What do they say about my love for her?
What do they expect from it?

PAULINUS

You can do what you please—love—cease to love;
The Court will think as you and take your part.

TITUS

Yes, I have seen that Court, and close at hand,
That Court too careful to applaud its Master;
I've seen that Court approve the crimes of Nero,
Go on their knees to him, and consecrate him.
Idolatrous courtiers shall not be my judge;
I will not lend my ear to flatterers.
I wish to know, from you, what people say.
You promise this. Respect and fear for me
Keep all complaints from coming to my ears.
Now, dear Paulinus, let me see and hear;
Be you my ears and eyes, interpret for me
The varying hearts of all my countrymen;
Let your sincerity bring truth to me
Across all lies, beyond all flattery.
Now speak! What ought Queen Berenice to hope?
Will Rome be cruel or indulgent to her?
Will Rome be angry if so fair a Queen
Be raised as Empress to the throne of Cæsar?

PAULINUS

Lord, there can be no doubt, whate'er the cause,
Be it reason or caprice, Rome does not want her

To be the Empress here.   They say, of course,
That she is good and beautiful, and seems
Made to be Empress over human beings;
They say she has a truly Roman heart,
And has a thousand virtues; but, my Lord,
You know the rest.   Rome, by unchanging law,
Will have no foreign blood mixed with her blood,
Will recognize no children born of marriage
Made against Roman custom, Roman law.
Besides, you know, in banishing her Kings
Rome took a hatred to the name of King.
Though Rome is faithful to the race of Cæsars,
That hate of Kings and Queens is furious still.
For Julius Cæsar longed for Cleopatra,
But dared not marry her.   She was a Queen.
Mark Antony, who made an idol of her,
Dared never marry her.   And since that time
Caligula and Nero, monstrous men,
Who stamped beneath their feet the laws of Rome,
Still feared that law, and did not dare to make
Marriages hateful to the Roman heart.
You have commanded me to be sincere—
Well, in the East, a slave, whom you set free,
A man still half a slave, a branded man,
Marked with hot irons, Lord, the freed man Pallas,
Married two Queens of Berenice's blood;
And do you think that you could marry her
Without outraging Rome while men know that?
You, marry her, while three days' sail from Rome
A branded slave, freed from our fetters lately,
Marries her relatives!
That is what Romans think about your love.
It may well be that ere this evening comes
The Imperial Senate's self will come to you,
To tell you all that I have told you now.

To say that Rome falls at your very feet
And asks that you should make another choice
More worthy her and you.
You might be thinking of your answer, Lord.

TITUS

Alas! they ask me to give up myself.

PAULINUS

It is a bitter struggle, I confess.

TITUS

Bitterer a thousand times than you can think.
It has been very life to see her here,
Each day to see her, love her, and to please her.
I have a hundred times given thanks to God
For bringing all the East beneath my Father
And putting bleeding Rome into his hands.
I have desired my dead Father's place,
Much as I loved him,
In hope of making Berenice Empress.
And now, Paulinus, when the time has come,
In spite of all my love and all her beauty,
In spite of all my lover's oaths and tears,
Now that I have Imperial power to crown her,
Now that I love her deeper than before,
Now that a happy marriage might unite us
After five years of prayers and hopes and love,
After all these, Paulinus—Oh, ye gods!

PAULINUS

What is it, Lord?

TITUS
                    I part from her for ever.

If I have made you speak to me to-day,

It was because I wished that your great friendship
Should help to kill my love which dies most hard.
Believe me, it is hard to conquer love;
My heart will bleed for more than one day yet.
My love was peace in those first days of love,
When still my Father was the Emperor,
I was the master of my fate and free,
Accounting to myself for my desires;
But when the gods recalled my Father to them,
My pleasant error was removed from me;
I felt the heavy load imposed upon me;
I knew that presently I should be forced
To give up self and all the loves of self,
And do the Will of God and not my own,
And give my life to work, not to myself.
And now, to-day, Rome watches what I do.
Shameful to me and ominous to her
If my first act should scatter every custom
And build my happiness on broken law.
I have resolved to make this sacrifice;
But how prepare Queen Berenice for it?
How can a man begin?
These last eight days full twenty times I've tried
To tell her this,
But at the first word my poor stumbling tongue
Seemed frozen in my mouth, I could not speak.
I hoped my sorrow and anxiety
Might make her feel our common misery;
But she has not suspected and knows nothing.
Now I have gathered all my constancy,
Now I must see her and must tell her all.
Now I am waiting for Antiochus:
I shall give him the prize I cannot keep,
And bid him take her back into the East.
He will leave Rome to-morrow with the Queen,

And I shall see her now and tell her this,
I shall now speak to her for the last time.

PAULINUS

Lord, I expected this from your great glory;
I knew your heart would not destroy its work,
That you, the conqueror of so many nations,
Would conquer all your passions if you willed.

TITUS

Glory is cruel under its fine names;
My sad eyes find her lovelier than glory.
If I have dared the death in seeking glory,
It was because her beauty lit in me
A longing for all lovely, splendid things.
You know quite well I did not always have
Renown or glory. I'd an evil name,
My youth was spent within the Court of Nero
And followed ways I love not to recall.
It was my seeing her that changed my life,
And to please her I loved, I did strange things
And came back triumphing. But blood and tears
Were not sufficient to win love from her,
So then I undertook to help the wretched.
I was more happy than my tongue can say
When she was pleased with work that I had done.
I owe her everything, and as reward,
Reward for all the good that she has done me,
I shall say "Go, and never see me more."

PAULINUS

Sir, do you fear that she will think you faithless?
The very Senate is surprised to think
How many honours you have given the Queen.
You have given her magnificence of power,

Up to Euphrates you have made her Queen
Over a hundred peoples.

Titus

But petty solace for a grief so great.
I know the Queen; I know only too well
That she has asked for nothing but my heart.
I loved her, she loved me; and since that day—
I cannot say if it were glad or sorry—
Her life has had no object but her love.
Unknown at Court, a stranger here in Rome,
She passes all her days with no more thought
Save that she see me some time, and the rest
Expect to see me.
And if, as sometimes happens, I am late,
I find her weeping.
All that there is most powerful in love—
Joy, beauty, glory, virtue, are in her.
For five long years each day that I have seen her
Has given me the joy the first sight had.
Let's think no more, because the more I think,
The more my made up mind shakes in its purpose.
Once more, once more, one must not think about it.
I know my duty and must follow it,
Whether I live or die is no great matter.

(*Enter* Rutilius.)

Rutilius

My lord, Queen Berenice would speak with you.

Titus

Paulinus—

Paulinus

So, Lord, you seem all ready to draw back.
Remember all your noble plans; it's time.

TITUS

Well, let us see her.   Let her enter there.

(*Enter* BERENICE.)

BERENICE

Do not be vexed if with a too great zeal
I break the secret of your solitude.
While the Court rings with all your gifts to me,
Would it be right were I to hold my peace?
Your mourning time is past; you are alone,
And none can hinder you; and yet, my Lord,
You do not come to see me as of old.
I hear you offer me another crown,
Yet hear it not from you.   Give me more love,
Give me less glory, Lord.   Can your love show
Only through orders of the Senate, then?
Ah, Titus! what new care does your love bring me?
Can it give naught but princedoms?   Ah!   Since when
Have you believed that greatness touches me?
A look, a sigh, a word out of your mouth,
Makes the ambition of a heart like mine.
See me more often, do not give me things.
Are all your moments given to the Empire?
After eight days have you no word to say?
Lord, reassure my trouble with a word.
Did you then speak of me when I surprised you?
Lord, was I at the least within your thought?

TITUS

Doubt it not, Lady.   I attest the gods
That you are ever present in my thought.
I swear that never absence, self, nor time,
Can tear you from this heart that worships you.

BERENICE

You swear eternal worship, but you swear

Most coldly. Why bring in the gods to witness?
Did you want oaths to overcome mistrust?
My heart does not contain mistrust of you;
I should believe you on a simple sigh.

TITUS

Lady!

BERENICE

Well, Lord? But what, you do not answer.
You turn your eyes and seem confounded, Sire.
Can you not see me, save with looks of grief?
Does your mind always mourn your Father's death?
Can nothing charm away this eating care?

TITUS

Would God my Father lived still,
I'd be happy!

BERENICE

Lord, this mourning
Justly proceeds from piety; but now
You have paid tribute to his memory
Enough; you owe now other cares to Rome.
I dare not speak to you about myself,
But formerly I could bring peace to you,
And you have listened to me even with pleasure.
You mourn a father still (alas, poor grief!)
While I, the memory makes me shudder still:
They would have dragged me from the man I love,
Dragged me, whose broken-heartedness you know
When you have left me even for a day.
I think that I should die upon the day
That they forbade me see you.

TITUS

Lady, alas! what do you say to me?

What time is this for speech? For pity, stop!
I am unworthy and your goodness kills me.

BERENICE

Unworthy, Lord? How could you be?
Does what you call my goodness weary you?

TITUS

No, Lady, never. But since I must speak,
My heart seems burning in a living fire.

BERENICE

Go on.

TITUS

Alas!

BERENICE

Speak!

TITUS

Rome, the Empire—

BERENICE

Well?

TITUS

We'll go, Paulinus—I cannot speak to her!

(*Exit* TITUS *and* PAULINUS.)

BERENICE

What, leave me thus and never say the reason!
What fatal thing is this? What have I done?
What does he want? What does this silence mean?

PHENICE.

It seems more strange the more one thinks on it.
Does anything come to your memory
That might have prejudiced him against you, Lady?

BERENICE

Believe me, dear,
When I recall the memories of the past,
From when I saw him first to this sad day,
Loving him well has been my only fault.
Could I have said a thing that has displeased him?
Have I with too much warmth returned his gifts?
Or blamed his depth of mourning for his Father?
Or is it that he fears the hate of Rome?
He fears, perhaps; he fears to wed a Queen!
Alas! if that were true,—but no! so often
He has declared to me a hundred times
His love is stronger than their cruel laws—
A hundred times. He must explain his silence.
I cannot live in this uncertainty;
I could not live, thinking that I had hurt him,
Or that he did not care. Wait, let me think!
Now that I think, it seems explained to me.
He knows the love of King Antiochus,
Perhaps that vexes him. And I was told
That he expects Antiochus even now.
Let us not seek elsewhere the explanation;
Doubtless the trouble that alarms him so
Is but a light suspicion easily killed.
Would Heaven, Titus, that a rival came,
A man more powerful than you, to tempt me,
To put more Empires at my feet than you,
To buy my love with sceptres numberless,
While you had nothing for me but your love—
Ah! then, dear Titus, you would see the price
I put upon my heart. But come, Phenice,
Let us be quiet, for he loves me still,
And I do wrong to count myself unhappy.
If he be jealous, 'tis a sign of love.

CURTAIN

ACT III

(TITUS, ANTIOCHUS, ARSACES.)

TITUS

So you are going, Prince? What sudden cause
Presses your going? (One might call it flight.)
You hide from me until you say good-bye.
Come, do you leave us as an enemy?
What will the Court, what will the Empire say?
Come! as your friend, have you a grudge against me?
Have I neglected you in all this crowd
Of Kings and Sovereigns pressing in the Court?
You were my friend during my Father's life,
Friendship was all I had to give you then.
Now, when my friendship has so much to give,
You fly from me.
Come, can you think that I forget old friends
And think about my greatness more than them,
And cast them off as things of no more use?
Prince, you are more than ever needful to me.

ANTIOCHUS

I, Lord?

TITUS

Yes, you.

ANTIOCHUS

Alas, Sir, what can you expect but prayer
From an unhappy Prince?

TITUS

Prince, I remember that my victory
Owed half its glory to your gallant deeds.
Rome has seen many of your captives pass,
And in the Capitol the spoils you took
Even from the Jews.

Now I expect from you no deeds of war,
Only your voice. I know that Berenice
Counts you her one true friend now here in Rome;
You, only, make one heart and soul with us.
Now, in the name of this most constant friendship
I bid you use the power you have upon her.
See her on my behalf.

ANTIOCHUS

I? See the Queen?
Sir, I have said farewell to her for ever.

TITUS

See her but once again for me, Antiochus.

ANTIOCHUS

Lord, you must speak to her. She worships you.
Why rob yourself of such a charming task?
Sir, she is waiting for you with impatience.
I answer, Sir, for her obedience.
She herself told me, she will marry you:
You need but see her, Sir, for she is won.

TITUS

Time was, so sweet a speech would have seemed sweet;
I should have been most happy. Even to-day
I thought to be most happy; yet to-day
I have to leave her, Prince.

ANTIOCHUS.

Leave her? You, Lord?

TITUS

Such is my destiny.
This is no marriage day for her and Titus;
I pleased myself in vain with that sweet hope.
Now, Prince, to-morrow she must sail with you.

Antiochus

O Heaven! what do I hear?

Titus

Pity my greatness!
Being Master of the world, I rule her fortune;
I can make Kings and then can unmake them,
And yet my heart is not my own to give.
Rome, ever bitter against Kings, disdains
An Empress born in the purple with a crown
And all a hundred Kings for forefathers.
My heart is free to love some common woman,
Rome would with pleasure see me marry one,
Even the most worthless in the city bounds—
Even Julius Cæsar bowed to this decree.
To-morrow, if she still be here, the Romans
Will come in fury here to bid her go.
Spare her this insult.   Since we must surrender,
Let us surrender finely.
My eight days' silence and my absence from her
Must have prepared her for this cruel speech.
Now at this very time she waits for me
To tell her of the trouble of my heart.
Now spare my heart the pain of telling her.
Go to her and explain my misery:
Above all, beg that I may keep from her.
Be the one witness of her tears and mine,
Take to her my farewells and bring me hers;
But let us both avoid that deadly meeting
That would destroy our last poor constancy.
And if the hope that I shall always love her
Can make the bitterness of parting less,
Swear to her, Prince, I shall be always faithful
And carry to my grave my love for her.
My reign will be a long, long banishment

If Heaven, not content with taking her,
Pains me still farther with a long, long life.
You, who are only linked to her by friendship,
Do not abandon her in her distress,
And let her going back into the East
Be glorious like a triumph, not a flight.
And may your friendship last; and let my name
Be often in your quiet talks together.
Your Kingdoms shall henceforward touch each other,
And the Euphrates be your boundary.
The Senate will confirm this by a vote.
I join Cilicia to your Comagena.
Good-bye! And do not leave my lovely Queen.
She was the one desire of my heart,
The one thing I shall love till my last breath.

(Exit Titus.)

ARSACES

So Heaven does justice to you! You will go,
But she'll go with you. Heaven does not take her,
But gives her.

ANTIOCHUS

　　　　　　Give me the time to breathe!
It is too great a change and I am shaken:
All that I love is put into my hands—
Can I believe what I have heard just now?
And if I can believe, should I be glad?

ARSACES

But, my great Lord, what can I think of you?
What barrier is there to your happiness?
A little while ago you came from here
All shaken from your last farewells with her,
Going, because her marriage broke your heart.
And now the marriage is the broken thing,
So what can grieve you now? Go where love calls you.

Antiochus

Arsaces, I am charged to take her home.
For a long time I shall be close to her;
It may be that in time her heart will change
And think my perseverance something sweet.
Titus o'erwhelms me here with all his greatness:
No one can be compared to him in Rome;
But in the East the Queen may count me something.

Arsaces

Doubt it not, Lord, all happens as you wish.

Antiochus

Ah! how we glory to deceive ourselves!

Arsaces

And why, "deceive ourselves"?

Antiochus

Ah! I might please her.
Might it not be that she would hear my love?
Among her woe, neglected by the world,
Might she not turn to me and stoop to me
For help that she would know my love would render?

Arsaces

Who could console her better than yourself?
Her fortune changes. Titus flings her off.

Antiochus

Alas, for that great change! Now I shall know
Even from her tears how much he loves him, friend.
For I shall see her weep, and pity her.
The only fruit of love that I shall gather,
Tears, which are not for me.

Arsaces

Why do you thus delight to wound yourself?

Did ever a brave heart show such a weakness?
Open your eyes, my Lord, and bravely think
How many reasons make the Queen your own.
Since Titus from to-day has cast her off,
Think thus. The Queen is forced to marry you.

ANTIOCHUS

Forced?

ARSACES

Yes. But grant her, first, some days for tears;
Let her first rush of sorrow run its course,
Then all will speak for you; her hate, her vengeance,
Absence of Titus, presence of yourself,
Time, and three kingdoms that she cannot rule—
Your kingdoms side by side, the better joined.
Interest, reason, friendship, all things bind you.

ANTIOCHUS

I breathe again. You give me life, Arsaces,
It is a happier prospect. Why delay?
Let us perform what we are bidden do.
We'll find the Queen, and, since the Emperor bids,
Tell her that Titus now abandons her.
No; stay! What am I doing? Can I do it?
I take this cruel task? My heart shrinks from it.
The lovely Berenice to hear from me
That she is cast aside! Unhappy Queen!
Who could have thought that this would be your fate?

ARSACES

Her anger will not fall on you, but Titus.
You only speak at his request, my Lord.

ANTIOCHUS

No, we'll not see her; we'll respect her grief.
Plenty will come to tell her of her fall.

Do you not think she will be sad enough
To learn to what contempt Titus condemns her,
Without this final thrust, to have the news
By Titus' only rival?   Let us go.
By going thus we shall escape her hatred.

ARSACES

Sir, here she comes! Think what to do and say.

ANTIOCHUS

O Heaven!

(*Enter* BERENICE.)

BERENICE

So, Lord, you are not gone?

ANTIOCHUS

Lady, I see you looked for Cæsar here.
Blame only Cæsar if you find me here
In spite of my farewells.
Perhaps by this I should have been in Ostia,
Had he not strictly ordered me to stay.

BERENICE

He wanted you alone.   He avoids us.

ANTIOCHUS

He only kept me here to speak of you.

BERENICE

Of me, Prince?

ANTIOCHUS

Yes.

BERENICE

What could he have to say?

ANTIOCHUS

Thousands of other men could tell you better
Than I.

BERENICE

What do you mean?

ANTIOCHUS

O be not vexed!
Others at such a moment might not keep
Silence so well, but would rejoice, perhaps,
Would swell with pride and joy to break the news;
But I, still trembling; I, as you know well,
Reckoning your quiet dearer than my own,
Would rather vex you than distress you, Queen.
I fear your sorrow more than your annoyance.
Before to-night you will acquit me, Queen.
Lady, good-bye.

BERENICE

But what strange speech! O stay!
O Prince, I cannot keep my grief from you.
You see before you a distressful Queen,
Whose heart seems killed, who only asks two words.
I think you said you feared to vex my quiet,
And therefore will not speak.
Lord, if my peace of mind be precious to you,
If I were ever precious in your eyes,
Lighten the darkness that is on my soul.
What did the Emperor say to you?

ANTIOCHUS

O, Lady,
For God's sake!

BERENICE

Is my heart's wish so little to you, then?

ANTIOCHUS

And if I speak, you will forever hate me.

BERENICE

I beg you speak. I order you to speak.

ANTIOCHUS

O gods!
Lady, once more, you'll wish I had not spoken.

BERENICE

Prince, either calm my mind by speaking now,
Or be assured that here our friendship ends.

ANTIOCHUS

Queen, after that, I cannot remain silent.
So, since you wish it, I will break the news.
Have no illusions now. For I shall tell you
Miseries, perhaps, of which you dared not think.
I know your very heart. Now be prepared,
For I shall strike your heart's most tender place.
Titus has ordered me. . . .

BERENICE

What has he ordered?

ANTIOCHUS

To say to you, that you . . . that you and he . . .
That you and he must separate, forever.

BERENICE

Separate? What? Who? I and he, you say?

ANTIOCHUS

Lady, let be. I must be just to him.
All that a loving and a generous heart
Could hold of wild despair in its worst moment,

Was there in Titus' heart. He wept. He loves you.
But little serves it if he love you still:
The Roman Empire dreads to have a Queen,
So you must separate. You go to-morrow.

BERENICE

Go! Misery! Phenice!

PHENICE

          Ah, blessed Lady,
This is a bitter blow! It daunts your soul.
Show your soul's greatness.

BERENICE

Titus to leave me after all his vows,
Titus, who swore to me! I cannot think it!
He cannot leave me.
Perhaps they turn his innocent mind against me,
Some trap is made to tear us from each other,
For Titus loves me, he does not wish my death.
Go now and see him, I would speak with him.
Go!

ANTIOCHUS

And you could look at me, and think that I—

BERENICE

You long for this too well to persuade me.
Know, I do not believe you. But true or false,
Keep you forever from my sight henceforth.
Do not you leave me, Phenice, I am faint.
Help me, good Phenice, put your arm here—so.

          (*Exeunt* BERENICE *and* PHENICE.)

ANTIOCHUS

Do I deceive myself? I heard her rightly?
"Keep me forever henceforth from her sight!"

I think I shall, for should I not have gone
Had Titus not against my will restrained me?
She thought to hurt me, but her hate has helped me.
You saw me going sick with hopeless love,
Jealous and in despair and wild of head;
And now, Arsaces, after this dismissal
Perhaps I may set out with resignation.

ARSACES

No, Lord; that less than ever. You must stay.

ANTIOCHUS

I stay? To see myself disdained!
See myself punished for the guilt of Titus!
With what injustice and indignity
She doubted of my truth.
She said that Titus loved her, I betrayed her!
Ungrateful Queen, to reckon me a traitor!
At such a time, too; at the fatal moment
When I was telling of my rival's sorrow.
When to console her I had made him seem
Loving and true, more than he is, perhaps.

ARSACES

Lord, what a pain you take to grieve yourself!
Let her grief go. Let its first anguish pass,
For in a week or month it will be passed.
Stay till it passes.

ANTIOCHUS

No, I go, Arsaces.
All things excite me to be gone from here,
So let us go. And for a long, long time
Let us not speak of her.
The day is not yet over. Go now, you;
See if her grief has not brought death to her.

Run!   I will wait until you come to me;
We'll know if she's alive before we start.

CURTAIN.

ACT IV

BERENICE

Phenice is late.   How slowly the time passes!
The bitter time!   My strength is going from me.
Yet rest seems death to me.   How late Phenice is!
It is ill-omened, and it frightens me.
It means that she will have no message for me,
That cruel Titus has not heard her speak,
But flies from her.

[Enter PHENICE.)

Dear Phenice, have you seen the Emperor?
What did he say?   When will he come?

PHENICE

                          I saw him, Lady,
Told him the trouble of your soul, and saw
His tears.

BERENICE
And is he coming?

PHENICE
Doubt not, madam,

He's coming; but you cannot see him thus;
You are disordered, madam; calm yourself,
And let me raise these fallen veils of lawn
And scattered hairs with which your eyes are hidden,
And marks of tears.

Berenice

No, leave them, Phenice; he shall see his work.
What use are these vain ornaments to me?
If all my love and tears and sighs and sorrow—
Nay, if my certain death can call him not,
How shall these useless helps of beauty call him?
They do not call him now.

Phenice

Why be unjust?
I hear a noise—the Emperor is coming.
Let us go in; we must avoid his courtiers,
See him alone, within.

(They *go off.*)

(*Enter* Titus, Paulinus *and* Company.)

Titus

Go to the Queen, Paulinus.   I will see her.
Leave me alone a little while; now go.

Paulinus

(*Going.*)

I fear this seeing the Queen!
Gods, save his glory and the country's honour.
Now for the Queen!

(*Exit* Paulinus.)

Titus

(*Alone.*)

Titus, the time has come; what will you do?
Have you prepared farewells, and steeled your heart
And braced it to the pitch of cruelty?
For in this bitter struggle now prepared
You need not bravery, but barbarism.
Now you will see her beauty all in tears;
And seeing that, can I fulfil my duty,
And break the heart I love, the heart that loves me,

And cast her off forever?
Why should I break that heart? Who bids me? I do.
Yet why? Has Rome declared her wishes to me?
Does the mad rabble roar around the palace?
And do I see the State at the cliff's brink?
And can I only save her by this yielding?
All's quiet here, and I, too swift, too swift
To torture self, perhaps imagine evils
That I could thrust aside.
Is there no other means but this to save it?
Would they not see the virtue of the Queen?
Would they not presently confess her Roman?
After such tears and love and faithfulness
Rome would be kind to us.—Ah, no! not Rome!
Hatred of Kings is stamped in every soul,
And cannot be effaced by fear or love.
Rome, casting out her Kings, condemned your Queen.
Coward I am. I love. Give up the Empire,
Go to the wide world's end, and live with her;
Make place for those more fit than I to reign.
Yes, but are these those deeds in the great style,
That were to crown me in men's memories?
Now I have reigned eight days, and till this day
I have done all for love, nothing for honour.
Now I must do what honour asks of me
And break the only link that hinders me.

(*Enter* BERENICE.)

BERENICE

Leave me, I say! you cannot keep me back,
I must speak with him. So, Lord, you are here!
Well, is it true that Titus casts me off?
That we must part, that Titus orders it?

TITUS

Lady, have pity on a wretched Prince.

We must not here give way to tenderness;
I have sufficient bitterness at heart
Without your tears to torture me still more.
Recall that heart, which many times of old
Showed me my duty; for the time has come;
But by your love, look simply at my duty
And fortify my heart against yourself,
And help me overcome my love for you.
Duty demands that we must separate.

BERENICE

You tell me this! I felt sure that you loved me!
My soul that loved you only lived for you.
Were you then ignorant of your Roman laws
When for the first time I confessed my love?
Why did you not, then, say "Oh, wretched Queen,
There is no hope! Why pledge your love to me?
Give not your heart to one who cannot take it."
But no, you took it, but to fling it back,
When that poor heart was living but for you.
Full twenty times they have conspired against us:
Then was the time—why not have cast me then?
There were a thousand things against me then
That might have helped console me in my grief.
I could have blamed your Father, all the Romans,
The Senate and the Empire, all the world,
Rather than this dear hand.
I should not then have had this cruel blow,
Even when I hoped to be most happy here.
Here, when your love can do all that it wishes
When Rome is silent and your Father dead
And all the world is bowing at your feet—
When I have nothing more to fear— then you—
You spurn me.

Titus

It was myself who thus destroyed myself,
I was content to live, to let myself
Be charmed; my heart would never search the future
For what might one day disunite us two.
I willed that nothing should o'ercome my wishes.
Examined nothing, hoped the impossible;
Perhaps for death rather than these farewells.
The very obstacles increased my love.
And Empire spoke but glory had not spoken
As yet, within my heart, in the clear tone
With which it stirs the hearts of Emperors.
I know the torments that this parting brings,
I know too well I cannot live without you.
But this is not a question now of living;
I have to reign.

Berenice

Then reign, harsh King, and be content with glory.
I will not vex you. No; I only waited
Before I would believe that those same lips
After a thousand oaths of love for me,
Would order me away for evermore.
I wished to hear you say it in this place.
Now nothing more. Good-bye for ever, then.
For ever, Sir, it is a cruel word
When one's in love.
A month will come, a year will come, and we—
We shall be parted by a world of seas.
How shall we suffer when the day begins
And the sun climbs the sky and then declines,
And Titus will not see his Berenice.
And all day long she will not look on Titus!
Perhaps you will not feel those days so long;
They may be long for me, too short for you.

Titus

Lady, I shall not live for many days;
I hope that presently news of my death
Will show you that I cannot live without you,
Will make you own, that you were loved indeed.

Berenice

If that be true, why should we separate?
I do not speak of marriage with you now:
Rome has condemned me not to see you more:
But do you envy me the air you breathe?

Titus

You can do all things, Lady. Stay, if you wish;
I'll not forbid it; but I feel my weakness;
It would be endless struggle, endless fear,
And endless watching to restrain my steps
From turning towards your beauty all day long.
I cannot speak, my heart forgets itself,
Remembering only that it loves you dearly.

Berenice

Well, Lord, and what could happen if I stayed?
Would all your Romans rise against me, Lord?

Titus

Who knows? Suppose they did? Suppose they clamoured?
I should be forced to back my choice by blood;
And if they did not speak and did not rise,
They would expect that some day I should pay them.
What would they not demand for their complaisance?
How can I guard the laws I cannot keep?

Berenice

You count the tears of Berenice for nothing?

TITUS

That is unjust.

BERENICE

Unjust? For unjust laws, that you can change,
You would condemn yourself to lifelong grief.
You say Rome has her rights. Have you not yours?
And are Rome's interests dearer than our own?
Come, speak!

TITUS

Alas, my Queen, you torture me!

BERENICE

You are the Emperor, Lord, and yet you weep.

TITUS

Yes, Lady, it is true. I weep. I shudder.
When I accepted here the Emperor's purple,
Rome made me swear to maintain all her laws.
I must maintain them. Already many times
Rome has most strictly proved her Emperors;
They have obeyed her orders to the death
To their sons' deaths. Rome and the glory of Rome
Have won the victory in those Roman hearts;
And I, in leaving you, do as they did,
But think I pass them in austerity.

BERENICE

All things seem easy to your barbarism.
I will not speak again of staying here.
Think you I would have wished, ashamed, despised,
To stay among the mocks of those who hate me?
Do not expect me to break out against you,
But if the gods have pity of my tears,
And if your harsh injustice touches them,
And if before I die I, the sad Queen,

Wish for some bold avenger of my death,
I seek that bold avenger in your heart—
My love, my love that cannot be effaced,
My present grief and my past happiness,
Are the enemies that I will leave you, Lord.
I leave my vengeance unto them. Good-bye.

(*Exit.*)

PAULINUS

Lord, she has gone. Will she then leave the country?

TITUS

Paulinus, follow her. I think she is dying.
Run to her help.

PAULINUS

My Lord, her women will be round her there,
They'll turn her thoughts. Fear not, the worst is over.
Go on, my Lord, the victory is yours:
I know you could not hear her without pity;
I couldn't keep from pity even in seeing her—
But you must take long views, and you must know
That happiness will come from this brief pain:
All the wide world will ring with praise of you.

TITUS

I hate myself! I am a brute! Even Nero
Was not so cruel. Oh, I cannot bear it!
If Berenice should die!
Come, let Rome say what it may.

PAULINUS

What, Lord?

TITUS
I know not what I say.
Excess of trouble overwhelms my spirit.

PAULINUS

Do not be troubled for what Rome will say.
The news that she has gone is spread abroad;
Rome, which was murmuring, is triumphing,
The altars are all smoking in your honour,
And in the streets the crowd, singing your virtues,
Crown all your statues with eternal laurel.

TITUS

Ah, Rome! Ah, Berenice! Unhappy fate,
To be a lover and an Emperor!

(Enter ANTIOCHUS *and* ARSACES.)

ANTIOCHUS

What have you done, my Lord? For Berenice
Is perhaps dying in Phenice's arms—
Hears and knows nothing, but cries out for death;
And you alone, my Lord, can save her life.
Lord, why delay? Go, show yourself to her,
And speak one word.

TITUS

     And what word can I say?

(Enter RUTILIUS.)

RUTILIUS

Lord, all the Tribunes, both the Consuls, and
The Conscript Fathers of the Roman Senate,
With one voice in the State's name call for you.
A great impatient crowd is with them, Lord;
They wait your presence in your audience chamber.

TITUS

I hear you. O great gods, I beg you save
That heart so like to die!

PAULINUS

Come, then, my Lord, we will attend the Senate.

ANTIOCHUS

Go to the Queen first.

PAULINUS

My Lord, you cannot! 'Twere indignity,
It were an insult to delay your coming,
Trampling the majesty of Rome beneath you.

TITUS

Enough, Paulinus, I will hear the Senate.

(Turns to ANTIOCHUS.*)*

Prince, this is duty not to be put by;
Go, see the Queen.   I hope on my return
She will not doubt my love.

CURTAIN

ACT V

ARSACES

Where shall I find this all too faithful Prince?
Heaven grant that at this moment I may tell him
Of happiness such as he dare not hope.
Oh, happy chance, he comes!   Sir, the Queen starts—

ANTIOCHUS

She starts?

ARSACES

She starts this evening.
She is most hurt that Titus leaves her there
So long in tears.   She is not angry now,
But she renounces Rome and Emperor both,
And would be gone before the Romans see her
In her distress, and glory in her flight.
She writes to Cæsar.

ANTIOCHUS

And Titus?

ARSACES

Titus has not appeared before the Queen,
For the great crowd of Romans rings him round,
Shouting the titles that the Senate gives him.
Those titles, and the crowd, and that applause,
Become so many honourable chains
To keep him from the Queen and steel his heart.
In spite of all the sad Queen's sighs and tears,
I think perhaps he will not see her more.

ANTIOCHUS

Fortune has played with me, and many times
I have seen all my plans blown by the wind;
My heart scarce hopes, lest it should anger Fortune.
But Titus comes.

(*Enter* TITUS.)

TITUS

Let no one follow me.
Prince, I am come to keep my promise here—
Come with a broken heart.　I wish to see her.

ANTIOCHUS

So dies the hope that you had given me!

(*Enter* BERENICE *and* PHENICE.)

BERENICE

I do not wish to hear.　My mind's made up;
I wish to go.　Why show yourself to me?
Why bring more bitterness to my despair?
Aren't you content?　I do not wish to see you.

TITUS

Please listen!

BERENICE

> The time's past.

TITUS

> Lady, a word!

BERENICE

No, not a word. You wish that I should go;
I am resolved to go, and I shall go.

TITUS

No, stay.

BERENICE

> Why should I stay?
To hear the people cheer for my misfortune?
Do you not hear their cruel joy already?
What have I done to them that they should cheer?
What have I done—save love yourself too well!

TITUS

It is a senseless crowd. Why listen to it?

BERENICE

There's nothing here that does not wound my heart.
This room where we were lovers, you and I,
Come, Phenice.

TITUS

> You are unjust to me.

BERENICE

You must go back, Lord, to the sacred Senate
Which now applauds you for your cruelty.
Are you content with what they say and vote?
And have you promised to forget my memory—
That will not expiate your love for me.
Have you made promise that you'll hate me always?

TITUS

No, I have promised nothing. O my gods!
Lady, for five years you and I have loved;
I never loved you better than to-day,
Never so tenderly, never so dearly.

BERENICE

"You loved," and yet at your command I go.
Do you find beauty in my heart's despair?
What use to me your heart's most useless love?
Show me less love for very pity's sake,
And let me at the least set forth persuaded
That I am leaving one who is not sad
To see me go.

(TITUS reads a letter.)

That is a letter that I wrote to you;
Read it, most cruel one, and let me go.

TITUS

You shall not go! I cannot grant you leave.
No, for your going is a strategem,
You mean to kill yourself, and all I love
Will be a bleeding memory.

(BERENICE falls upon a chair.)

Call for Antiochus.   Let him quickly come.
Lady, when first I knew we had to part,
I braced my soul for great unhappiness,
But did not once foresee the tiniest part
Of what I suffer now.
Some minutes since I met assembled Rome,
The Senate spoke to me, I did not hear,
I did not know if I were Emperor,
Or even a Roman, and I did not care.
Lady, I might say this: that I am ready
To give up Rome for you and follow you.

Even to the wide world's end to live with you.
But you yourself would blush if I said that,
You would not, without shame behold me so,
See me a worthless Emperor, without Empire,
March in your train, a spectacle to men.
No, to escape these torments of the soul
There is a nobler way, as you know well,
Which men too shaken by misfortune take
When sorrow upon sorrow following close,
Comes like a secret order to surrender.
If I be forced to watch your sorrow, lady,
If I be forced to see you long for death,
If I be forced always to dread your death,
As dread I must unless you swear to me
To spare your life, then look for other sorrow,
In this my state I can do anything.
I will not answer that my hand, before you
Put not a bloody end to this our parting.

BERENICE

Alas.

TITUS

No. There is nothing that I could not do.
So, madam, think that you control my life
And if I still am dear to you—

(*Enter* ANTIOCHUS.)

Come, Prince, come in!
I have sent for you to be my witness,
For to judge if I have loved untenderly.

ANTIOCHUS

Lord, you have honoured me with your esteem,
And I can tell you here, Lord, I have been
A faithful friend to you—
A faithful friend although I was a rival.

Titus

My rival!

Antiochus

　　　　　　Yes, it's time I told you that.
Lord, I have always worshipped Berenice,
Have striven to kill my love, but could not do it.
At least I could be silent, and I was.
Your change of heart gave me some feeble hope;
But the Queen's tears have wiped away that hope.
She asked to see you, and I called you, Lord,
And you came back. You love her. She loves you.
I pray the gods to keep their blows from you,
Or cast them upon me, whose life is yours.

Berenice

Too generous Princes, I am in despair!
Titus, you know my heart; I can say truly
I never longed for greatness nor for glory.
I loved!—I loved and wished to be beloved.
I thought your love had come unto its end.
I know my error now. I know you love me.
I am not worth your trouble, nor deserve
That marrying me your Empire should be broken.
I think that for five years until to-day
My love for you has been a real love.
That is not all. Now, in this fatal moment,
By a last effort I must crown the rest;
I shall obey your orders to the last.
Good-bye, Sir. Reign. I shall not see you more,
Prince, after this farewell, you must be sure
I cannot listen to another's love;
But live, and make an effort like our own.
I love him, he loves me, and yet we part.
Go, Sir, far from me, and forget your love.
Good-bye. We'll be example to all time

Of the most tender and unhappy love
That ever was in dolorous history.
All is made ready.   They are waiting for me.
No, follow not my steps.   Good-bye!
For the last time, good-bye, Lord.

(Exit.)

ANTIOCHUS

Woe is me!

CURTAIN.

A KING'S DAUGHTER
A TRAGEDY IN VERSE

A KINGS DAUGHTER

This play was performed at The Oxford Playhouse, on Friday and Saturday, May 25th and 26th, 1923, by the following cast of the Hill Players:

PERSONS

JEZEBEL, Queen of Samaria.................*Penelope Wheeler*
ROSE-FLOWER, First Chrous...............*Judith Masefield*
MOON-BLOSSOM, Second Chorus..................*Jean Downs*
HAMUTAL, The Steward's Wife..............*Paulise De Bush*
A PROPHET.......................................*Basil Maine*
JEHU, Captain of the Horse.....................*Ronald Hay*
MICAIAH, A Seer.........................*George G. Edwards*
AHAB, King of Samaria........................*Leslie Davey*
PHARMAS⎫ Court Attendants ⎰...........*Wilfred Messenger*
ASHOBAL⎭   ⎱.................*Henry Chapin*
NABOTH, A Farmer..........................*Dudley Barlow*
AHAZIAH, Crown Prince of Samaria...............*W. E. May*
JORAM, His Younger Brother...........*Wilfred Howe-Nurse*
ZAKKUR, Jehu's Messenger..................*H. G. Wakeford*
PASHUR, The Bringer of the News...........*C. E. J. Vincent*
ZIKRI ⎫ Spearmen ⎰.........................*F. J. Saunders*
KALLAI⎭   ⎱......................*Bernard Griffiths*

———

SCENE: The Palace in Samaria

———

A KING'S DAUGHTER

FIRST ACT

Jezebel

I am Queen Jezebel, King Ahab's wife.
I was princess in Sidon long ago,
But in an evil day I became Queen
Over these strangers in Samaria.

Here, for these last ten months, we fought the Syrians,
Till hope was gone; then, suddenly, all changed;
The Syrian army fell into our hands.

King Ahab had two choices: one, to kill
All of the Syrians; one, to let them go.
He made a peace with them and let them go.

Now all the people of this city rage
At Ahab, for his peace, and cry aloud
That I, the foreign queen with foreign gods,
Made Ahab make the peace to please my friends.

Four days ago, King Ahab sought to buy
A vineyard, from one Naboth, who refused
To sell the vineyard, even to his King.

To-day the rebels of the town prepare
A feast to Naboth for refusing him,
And at the feast the prophets and seditious
Will urge our murder as a godly deed.

What is King Ahab doing to defeat them?
Nothing. For these three days he has been hidden,
Brooding upon his bed in bitterness;
Refusing food and drink; refusing speech

With me, his wife; neglecting court and state;
Letting rebellion grow, and seeing no man
Except our younger son, evil Prince Joram,
Who longs for war against the Syrians.

So I, the Queen, not knowing what may come
When the King sickens and the people rage,
Have sent for help, called home our eldest son,
Prince Ahaziah, from his frontier post
With all his horsemen.   He should soon be here.

With Ahaziah and his horsemen here,
We shall be safer from our enemies,
The Teshbon prophet and the soldier Jehu,
The captain of the horse under the King.

*   *   *   *   *   *   *

Those are the enemies whom most I dread,
Lord Jehu and the Prophet, hand and mouth
To violence and unwise ways of life,
Violent and brainless both, as lightning is.

When violence and madness are in league,
Destruction comes.

                    And they are coming now,
Here to the palace of the King and Queen,
To plot their evil with our followers.

I will go hence, to pray that Ahaziah
May come in time to thwart their wickedness.

(*Exit*)

(*Enter the* PROPHET)

PROPHET

Lord Jehu!

(*Enter* JEHU)

JEHU

Ha, my Prophet!

PROPHET

Is all well?

JEHU

Yes. All goes well. This King, this imbecile,
This Ahab, still is sulking like a child,
Speaking with no one, making all things easy
For us, my Prophet, who will now succeed.
Nothing can stop us now. All works for us.
Ahab is hated; Jezebel detested;
The army sickened at their loss of plunder,
All hot against them both. Our only danger
Their son, Prince Ahaziah, far away,
Their other son, Prince Joram, working for us.
And now this feast to Naboth as a crown
To all these helps, an opportunity.

PROPHET

Truly our work is godly, since it prospers.
Since all is thriving, it is surely time
That we set forth together to this feast.

JEHU

Wait, yet, my Prophet, while I ask you this:
What objects will be served by this our feast?

PROPHET

Why, it will honour Naboth for resisting
The tyrant whom we hate, and give our friends
A chance to come together with Prince Joram
To cry aloud for war with Syria.

JEHU

True Prophet; "honour Naboth; cry for war;"
Such were our objects when we planned the feast:
That was the plan, but, friend, it is not now.
No, Prophet, no; for I have changed my mind.

This feast to Naboth which we have prepared
Must be the prelude to a mightier deed.
Prophet, I know thy zeal for true religion,
And you know mine; now, therefore, stand by me.
I am determined to be King this day.
The chances are all for me, and the feast
Puts them within my hand for me to take.
Now, therefore, Prophet, when you see me there,
Sitting at feast among the men-of-war,
Send out some youngling of the Prophet tribe
There to anoint me King in Ahab's stead.
Then I will rise and lead those men-at-arms
To end this Ahab and his Jezebel,
And stamp them with our horses' feet, and bring
A true religion back: by God, we need it.
No. Doubt not the success. Anoint me King,
The men will follow. For, by God, now, Prophet,
Look at my eyes, I mean this to succeed.
This is the way, because all other ways,
The way we planned before and any way,
Must end in this; so send the stripling to me.
Make me the King.

PROPHET

Truly a spirit speaks within you, Jehu.
Truly the devilries of Jezebel
Have brimmed the cup, and Ahab's treachery
Has spilled it over. You shall be the King.
Here with my blood, I do anoint you King.
My young man shall anoint you with the oil,
But will the captains follow you as King?

JEHU

They'll follow; some for plunder, some for fear.
Now let us to this Naboth's feast, to raise
Our following against this doting King.

PROPHET

Here is our friend Ashobal with some news.
(*Enter* ASHOBAL)

ASHOBAL

I was afraid that you had gone, Lord Jehu.
Prophet, Lord Jehu, there is danger here.
I have just heard from Jezebel's own lips
That she has ordered Ahaziah hither
With all his horse, and that he will be here
Within two hours.

PROPHET

Gods!

JEHU
Did Jezebel

Tell you of this?

ASHOBAL
No; I was hidden, and
I overheard her as she told her women.

PROPHET

She sent for them?

ASHOBAL

She said so.

PROPHET
But for what?
To be a bodyguard?

ASHOBAL
She did not say,
But that is what they will be when they come.

PROPHET

Then she suspects us.

ASHOBAL

Probably.

Jehu

The hag!

Prophet

These women of false gods shall die the death.

Jehu

Yes, unless we die first.   Thank you, Ashobal,
You bring the message in the nick of time.
Why has she sent for them?   Is Ahab dying?
No; he is ill, not dying.   By the gods,
The harlot may be plotting against Ahab
To crown her son?
No, by the gods, put by these pleasant dreams,
The likelier thing will be the explanation.
One of the little sheep within our fold
Has bleated to the shepherd: we have been
Betrayed, my Prophet and my sweet Ashobal,
Betrayed. . . . By whom?
By all the gods, this harlot is a man.
She hears of us, at once decides to strike,
Sends for the cavalry to cut our throats,
Calls Ahaziah to be King until
Her Ahab be a man again, and so
Bids for her husband's crown.   There are the facts.

Ashobal

Even so I judged it, from the way she spoke.

Prophet

Then we had better scatter into hiding,
For we are lost.

Jehu

True, brother Prophet, all our heads are loose,
But yet not lost.

PROPHET

But what are we to do?

JEHU

Stop Ahaziah in his coming here.
It can be done if he be two hours hence.
He must be coming by the desert road
Passing by Springs. Well, he shall meet his match.
Go, Prophet, to the feasting, as we planned.
Praise Naboth and be bitterer than spurge
About this peace. Pharmas must know of this.
Find Pharmas, that the Prophet speak with him.
Then tell what friends you can. Remember, Prophet,
Hold to our former plans till I return.
Now I must go.

(*Exit* JEHU)

PROPHET

And we had better go
Straight into hiding, while we have the time.

ASHOBAL

No, we must keep to what is planned and do
What Jehu tells us.

PROPHET

I must see Pharmas, then; find Pharmas for me.

ASHOBAL

I cannot yet.
Pharmas is in attendance on the Queen.

PROPHET

Why should he be with her, to-day of all days?
He is the King's attendant, not the Queen's.

ASHOBAL

True, but the Queen commanded him this morning

To write at her dictation; he will be
There, until noon; but it is nearly noon.

PROPHET

We are discovered by this Jezebel,
And Pharmas has betrayed us.

ASHOBAL

No, he is faithful to us.   Five years since
This Jezebel once chided him in public
For breaking of a cup.   He has remembered.
He swore to be revenged and means to be.
Now I say this: Come on the stroke of noon,
Here, to have speech with Pharmas and myself.
We may have news by then.   If the worst happen,
We shall have time enough for flight at noon.

PROPHET

You may be right; pray Heaven that you be.

ASHOBAL

Hark! there is someone coming through the court.
By heaven!

PROPHET

Why, who is it?   What has happened?

ASHOBAL

It is the King, recovered from his brooding
And dressed as for an audience with his peers.
If Ahab be in health again, why, death——

PROPHET

What shall we do?   Oh, say!

ASHOBAL

                    Be not found here.
He's coming hither with his man, Micaiah.
Go quickly, quickly.

                    (*Exit* PROPHET)

(Enter MICAIAH)

MICAIAH

Way for their Majesties! It is commanded
That all avoid. Way for their Majesties!
Avoid the room, Ashobal, for the King.

(Exit ASHOBAL)

(Enter AHAB)

AHAB

Micaiah, put my staff into my hands.
Go, now, desire the Queen to give me audience.

(Exit MICAIAH)

Thus does the climber on a pinnacle.
He stands exhausted on the peak and feels
Nothing beneath him but the mist of cloud
Hiding the precipice. I have my foothold;
Around me, the sheer fall into the pit.

(Enter JEZEBEL)

JEZEBEL

So, my good lord, at last I look upon you
After these days of anguish. O my lord,
What has afflicted you, that you should shut
Your doors upon me, send no word to me,
No word till now, not even let me know
If you were ill or well.

But no upbraiding.
Tell me what is the trouble of your soul.

AHAB

What do you think?

JEZEBEL

I know not what to think,

Living alone, shut from you, that should tell me.
Men say that you are grieved because a farmer,
One Naboth, would not sell his vineyard to you.

AHAB

I, grieved, at that?

JEZEBEL

I have no guide save rumour.

AHAB

His vineyard? Why, I did not want the vineyard.

JEZEBEL

Not want it, lord?

AHAB

Why should I want it; think?

JEZEBEL

I cannot think, indeed, why you should want it.

AHAB

Jehu was wanting it, to bring it in
Within the city wall, for in the siege
The Syrian archers shot our people from it.
Jehu demanded it.

JEZEBEL

        Jehu? Not you?
Yet do you know that men are cursing you
For wanting Naboth's land; and feasting Naboth
To-day, in public, for refusing you?
And that our crowns and even our lives are threatened?

AHAB

No, Queen, I do not know and cannot care.
What is the raging of the fools to me
Who ponder day and night upon a question,
A question that goes down into the bone
And burns like fire, till I cannot sleep

Or eat or work, for it is always here.
No, do not look like that, I am not mad,
Not yet; I am not mad. But always night and day
This question is about me and within me,
Haunting and harsh: the question, "Am I wrong?
Are these, my people who oppose my will,
Right, after all, righter than I, the King?
Righter throughout my twenty years of kingship?"

JEZEBEL

How can these preys to every passionate flaw
Be righter than an upright mind and conscience?

AHAB

I cannot tell, and yet I think they are.

JEZEBEL

You know they are not.

AHAB

No, I do not know.
I wonder, if the blunt and bawdy world
Be not the worse for wisdom, not the better.

JEZEBEL

It is a sin and cowardice to say so.

AHAB

Is it, my Queen? I wonder if it be.
Here have I striven twenty years, for peace
With Syria, and for liberty of thought
Within our borders, yet with what results?
Almost continual war with Syria,
Almost a civil war within this land.
Such being the fruits, I think the seeds were wrong.

JEZEBEL

The seeds were right, and if the fruit has failed,

Blame the bad soil, the bitter weather, drought,
Evil of many men hacking the plant,
All things, but you who planted, and the seed.

AHAB

Even if the seed were right, the ground was wrong.
And then I sowed it out of season, lady.
I could have smitten Syria to the dust,
Yet granted terms. I risked a civil war
To grant the terms. They do not keep the terms.
And these my people prefer blood to quiet.
And now I doubt the usefulness of wisdom,
Doubt my whole life; and wonder, if the prophets,
The people, and the bloody ways they love,
Be not indeed God's ways for governing.
If these things be, then I have failed my country.

JEZEBEL

O King, you cannot say that things are wrong
Because they fail. All good things seem to fail;
The road that men make is not straight nor smooth,
Nor like the perfect roadway that they planned;
And yet among the thorns and broken flint,
And twistings where the adder lies in wait,
It is a path where no path was before.
So with your Syrian pact and with these people,
You have hewed out a way where men will tread.
Be comforted and proud, for you have done it,
As the lone artist makes the perfect thing,
With every blind malignant saying "No!"
You have made peace as generous as yourself
And thought as free. So let the madman rave
And let the savage shriek for blood, and let
The blind worm of the many-creeping world
Crawl its obstruction, you have conquered them.

AHAB

It is not true. I have not conquered them.
They conquer me. I am defeated. Yes,
I cannot think, or master, or decide,
Having no longer any faith remaining
In what we planned together and have done.
The ground is gone from under me, the light
Is gone from in me, and the sky above
Is black with punishment that threatens me.
These ruffian prophets have been proven right,
Our policies have been accurséd; ay,
And the reward is death.

JEZEBEL

O husband, stay!

AHAB

I will not stay. The penalty is death,
With hell to follow, as the blind man's payment
Fully deserved.

(*Exit* AHAB)

JEZEBEL

Gods save us, he is mad, or over-wrought
Up to the point of madness; now, indeed,
We have been conquered, for we have no King,
Save one distraught with trouble. How am I
To help in this?

So ends my queenship with him. It is well
That I have called Prince Ahaziah home.
But, till he come, I govern, I am King,
And one act of a King must now be done:
This rebels' feast to Naboth must be stopped.

(*She claps her hands for* MICAIAH, *who enters*)

Micaiah, is there dust upon the road
To show the Prince's coming?

MICAIAH

Not yet, Madam.

JEZEBEL

How soon can he be here?

MICAIAH

                    Within two hours,
Unless he halt for noontide by the Springs.
He might be here much sooner.   Say, one hour.

JEZEBEL

Who is the captain of the guard to-day?

MICAIAH

Rechab, to-day, good lady.

JEZEBEL

                    Go, Micaiah,
Tell Pharmas that I wait him in the throne-room;
Bid him bring ink and seals; bid him be quick
Attend me there.

MICAIAH

Madam, I go.

                    (*Exit* MICAIAH)

JEZEBEL

Though the King sicken, it shall still be seen
That I, the Syrian woman, am a queen.

                    (*Exit* JEZEBEL)
                    (*Enter* PROPHET)

PROPHET

Pharmas! Ashobal! Hark! Is Pharmas there?
It is full noon, but Pharmas is not here.
No, nor Ashobal.   But there seems to be

Less danger than I feared: I was not questioned,
And men go unmolested to the feast.

(*Enter* ASHOBAL)

Here is Ashobal. Where is Pharmas, friend?

ASHOBAL

Gone to the Queen again, with ink and seals.
There is this news: the King and Queen have talked
And Ahab now is in his room again,
Moodily sharpening his sword, and muttering.
I myself think that Ahab has gone mad.

PROPHET

No word from Jehu yet, of Ahaziah?

ASHOBAL

None yet, nor will be for a while.

PROPHET

King Jehu,
Jehu, the King, God's comet, bringing change.
Come soon, come soon.   O what is Pharmas doing?

ASHOBAL

He writes some pressing matter for the Queen.

PROPHET

We shall be late. Come, Pharmas! Hurry, hurry!
Would he were here and we away from this.
We are like hunters in the lion's den,
Knowing the lion to be near.

ASHOBAL

I hear him.
Yes; this is Pharmas coming.   Here he is.

(*Enter* PHARMAS)

PROPHET

Pharmas, we have been waiting for you; come.
We must be going.   Listen to your orders.
During this feast go down among the guards. . . .

PHARMAS

Do not you talk of feasting, nor of guards.
The Queen has sent Micaiah with the guards
To fetch poor Naboth here.

ASHOBAL

Why?

PROPHET

What to do?

PHARMAS

I do not know; but not for any good.
"Fetch Naboth here before me," was the order.
It has gone off by this.

ASHOBAL

This is the end!

PROPHET

What can she want with Naboth?   Painted hag,
Thus to command a man.

ASHOBAL

Was the guard ordered to suppress the feast?

PHARMAS

No, but it is suppressed with Naboth taken.

ASHOBAL

We shall be taken next, so save yourself.

PROPHET

I will be gone.   You know my hiding-place,

The old one, near the wall; send word to me
There, if you have a message.

(Exit)

MICAIAH

Way for Her Majesty the Queen, make way!

(Enter MICAIAH)

Set forth the chair of audience for the Queen
Be reverent; the Queen approaches.   Hail!

(Enter JEZEBEL)

JEZEBEL

Micaiah, Pharmas and Ashobal, stay.
Within few moments, when the guards return,
You will return to take your places here,
Even as you stand this minute.

THE MEN

We will do so.

JEZEBEL

All three of you; you understand?

THE MEN

Yes, Madam.

JEZEBEL

Dismiss then, till the guards appear.

(The MEN go)

I am the King, upon whose balance lies
The nation's need to prompt me to be wise.
Ruin to all I cherish, if I fail.
God, judge for me, thy wisdom turn the scale.

CURTAIN

Rose-Flower

Once long ago young Nireus was the King
  In Symé Island, so the stories say,
  And at his birth the gods made holiday
And blessed the child and gave him each one thing.

Courage, and skill, and beauty, and bright eyes,
  Wisdom, and charm, and many another power,
  So that he grew to manhood like a flower
For beauty, and like God for being wise.

Now Nireus' friend was Paris, out of Troy,
  Paris, the prince, the archer, who had seen
  The goddesses within the forest green;
King Priam's son, a peacock of a boy.

Moon-Blossom

At Sparta's court, not far from Symé Isle,
  Bright Helen lived, King Menelaus' Queen,
  The loveliest woman that has ever been,
Who made all mortals love her by her smile.

Nireus and Paris went together there
  To Helen's palace; and when Nireus saw
  Helen the queen, the lovely without flaw,
He loved her like her shadow everywhere.

And Paris, when he saw her with her mate,
  Helen, the rose, beside that withered weed,
  Loved her no less, but with a young man's greed,
That wants the moon from heaven and cannot wait.

Rose-Flower

Straightway he wooed Queen Helen to be his,
  And won her love, and cried to Nireus then,
  "O Nireus, help to save us from this den,
Lend us your ship to bring us out of this."

So Nireus, though his heart was torn with pain,
   Well knowing what would come, yet took the pair
   To many-towered Troy and left them there,
To live in love and be the city's bane.

Moon-Blossom

When Menelaus knew of Helen's flight,
   He led all Greece in arms to punish Troy,
   Nireus went with him in the fleet, and joy
Ceased in the world, for all men went to fight.

Nine years they fought there in the tamarisk field,
   And in the tenth, in some blind midnight stour,
   Nireus killed Paris underneath the tower.
Men bore him back to Helen on his shield.

Rose-Flower

Then Troy was sacked and Menelaus took
   Beautiful Helen as his prisoner home,
   And locked her in his castle as a gnome
Might lock a gem on which no man might look.

Together

Thus Nireus lost his love, and killed his friend,
   And knew despair; so going to his ship,
   He sailed to where the constellations dip,
In the great west, to look for the world's end.

Rose-Flower

When Troy was sacked and all her towers
   Blazed up and shook into the sky,
Smoke like great trees and flame like flowers,
   And Priam's bodyguard did die.

Then the Queen's women snatched up spears
   And fought their way out of the gate,

Seized horses from the charioteers
   And fled like mountain-streams in spate.

They would not stay for slavery
   To some Greek lord until they died,
They rode the forest to be free
   Up on the peaks of snowy Ide.

Moon-Blossom

And in the forest on a peak
   They hewed a dwelling with the bronze,
And lived, unconquered by the Greek,
Fierce, sun-burned women, neither tame nor weak,
   The panther-women called the Amazons.

They lived there on the heights and knew no men.
   Having beheld the lusts of men destroy
   The town of windy Troy,
   They killed all men they met; their only joy
Was hunting for the wild beasts in the glen.

Together

The wild-boar and the many-branching stag,
   Horse-killing panthers hidden by the brook,
The spotted death among the yellow flag,
   All these with their bright spears these women took.
All these, and men, for even to be seen
By men, these hunter women thought unclean.

So no man saw them save a glimpse afar
   Of panther-skins flung back, and swift feet flying,
And the red stag brought low to the fierce Ha!
   Of women's spear-thrusts driven in the dying.
They ruled the crags like wolves, they kept their pride
Savage and sovereign like the snow on Ide.

SECOND ACT

MICAIAH

Madam, the soldiers have brought the farmer, Naboth; they have him in the guardroom, waiting for your orders.

JEZEBEL

Were you set upon as you brought him through the city?

MICAIAH

No, Madam, but a crowd followed, which is now at the palace gates.

JEZEBEL

Is it threatening?

MICAIAH

No, Madam, but uneasy.

JEZEBEL

Thank you, Micaiah. What standing has this Naboth?

MICAIAH

He lives in the city, but has this vineyard and some other ground, outside the walls. He is a small farmer, strict in religion. Nothing but religion will move him.

JEZEBEL

I will try whether that be true. Go now, without, and bring me Ashobal and Pharmas.

MICAIAH

I will, Madam.

(Exit)

JEZEBEL

If I can persuade this man to sell his land, then this gathering will lose all purpose. If he will not sell, as I doubt he will not, then, how then?

(MICAIAH, PHARMAS, ASHOBAL *enter*)

Stand where you are and pay especial heed
To what is said by us.

THE MEN

We will, great Queen.

JEZEBEL

I thank you.   Will you bring the man, Micaiah.

(*Enter* MICAIAH, *with* NABOTH, *crowned as for a feast*)

MICAIAH

Madam, your servant waits for your commands.

JEZEBEL

Thank you, Micaiah.   Keep in presence here.
You are that Naboth of the South-west Precinct?

(NABOTH *nods*)

Our calling of you here may come untimely.
You are at feast, or going to a feast?

NABOTH

I'm here; you've caught me; do the worst you can,
But do not mock me.

JEZEBEL

       I mock no one, Naboth.
I sent for you because I wished to speak
About the purchase of your vineyard near
The city wall.

NABOTH

Why do you want my vineyard, tell me that?

JEZEBEL

I do not want it.

NABOTH

Well, your husband does.

Jezebel

He does not, Naboth. Listen, all of you.
There is a false suspicion spread abroad
That we, the King and Queen, have coveted
This land of Naboth's. It is wholly false.
We do not want it, never wanted it,
But bid for it, on public grounds, because
Lord Jehu, captain of the bodyguard,
The overseer of the town's defences,
Urged, and still urges, that the vineyard be
Brought in, within the city wall. As King,
The King made offer for the land, through one. . . .
Which of you was it?

Ashobal

               I made the offer for His Majesty,
So please you, Madam.

Jezebel

Since it is not your rulers but your city
That needs the land, we ask you to consider
The giving up your holding to be walled.

Naboth

God pleased to put my vineyard where it is.
Why should you change it?

Micaiah

              In the siege, good Naboth,
The Syrian archers used to shoot from it
Into the city.

Naboth

            And they might again
Soon, in another siege?

Jezebel

So Jehu thought.

NABOTH

If you idolaters had done God's will
And killed these Syrians when God bade you kill,
You would have had no other siege to dread.

ASHOBAL

You must not speak this evil of your rulers.
Say nothing but as touching on the treaty.

JEZEBEL

Whether your land should be enclosed or no
I cannot tell: Duke Jehu says it should be;
Says that for public good it should be walled.
You would not sorrow that your land should go
For greater safety of your fellow townsmen?

NABOTH

I would.

JEZEBEL

I do not think you would, good sir.
Yet, if a war should follow and a siege
Threaten again, your vineyard would be taken
Maugre your will, and walled in spite of you
By public means; and you would lose it, so.

NABOTH

I would not lose it.   It would still be mine.

JEZEBEL

I cannot well see how; but let that be.
I ask you now to be content to treat
For this your plot.   May we proceed in this?

NABOTH

Dismiss your gang of killers here, these three
Lying in wait upon a poor man's words.

JEZEBEL

These are no killers, but my palace servants.
We are in treaty for exchange of land,
Or hope to be, and civil law prescribes
That sales of land be bargained before witness.

NABOTH

Where are my witnesses, to speak for me?

JEZEBEL

Well thought of, Naboth. Will you therefore send
To three, your friends, to witness to your words?

NABOTH

No, I will not.

JEZEBEL

Why not?

NABOTH

No matter why.
You have caught me, but catch my friends yourself
If you do want them.

JEZEBEL

Will you choose three men
Here in the palace, then, as witnesses?

NABOTH

I have a witness, stronger than your three,
Already present, woman of false gods.

ASHOBAL

Do not misname the person of your Queen.
You will lose all by rudeness. You have heard
That our great Queen demands to bargain with you,
But means no harm to you, nor to your friends.

JEZEBEL

Thank you, Ashobal.   (*Then to* NABOTH)

May we now proceed?

NABOTH

I have not yet agreed to treat with you.

JEZEBEL

You waste our time.   Speak.   Will you treat or not?

NABOTH

Before I treat, what do you offer for it?

JEZEBEL

What is its yearly value?

ASHOBAL

Seven casks.

MICAIAH

Madam, that may have been the yearly yield
In its best seasons, but it is not now.
It is no vineyard now, great Queen; the vines
Were routed up by Syrians in the siege.

JEZEBEL

So?   Did you know of this, Ashobal?

ASHOBAL

No.

JEZEBEL

Not know of it?

ASHOBAL

Not when I bargained for it.

JEZEBEL

Yet knew it now, and never mentioned it?
Would let me bargain for a vineless vineyard
As though it gave full vintage.

ASHOBAL

O good Madam,
You asked its yearly value, not its worth.

JEZEBEL

That shall be proved. Naboth, I did not know
That this your vineyard had been routed up.

NABOTH

That damned idolator, your husband, knew it.
He said that as it was not now a vineyard,
He could plant herbs there.

JEZEBEL

Bridle you your tongue.
When did His Majesty the King say this?
To whom?

NABOTH

It is well known he said it openly.

JEZEBEL

To you?

NABOTH

No.

JEZEBEL

Then to whom? To one of these?
You are all silent. Yet the King has seen
No other man, since his return to Shemer,
Except Prince Joram; therefore what you say
Is false in fact, seditious being said.
Ashobal, what was offered for the vineyard?

ASHOBAL

A better vineyard; then, that being refused,
Three vineyards, each one better, in full bearing,
Two of red grapes and one of white, O Queen.

JEZEBEL

And he refused?

MICAIAH

He did.

JEZEBEL (*To* NABOTH)

And do you still?

NABOTH

Yes.

JEZEBEL

Why?

NABOTH

Because the vineyards that he offered
Aren't his to offer.

JEZEBEL

       But they are, good Naboth.
They are the King's.

NABOTH

Does the King work them, then?

JEZEBEL

Yes, they are worked at his command.   How else?

NABOTH

His sweat does not fall on them.

JEZEBEL

       It has done so.
He with his own hands worked those vineyards, Naboth,
Before his father, Omri, became King,
As you well know.

NABOTH

I'll have no slave-tilled vineyard.

JEZEBEL

Men cannot live without the work of others;

You yourself do not. Did you make that robe,
Those shoes, that pouch? But we are wandering.
Let me, the Queen, make offer for your vineyard.
I offer the King's vineyards as before
And with them, the three marrowy olive-groves
Which Shemer planted.

NABOTH

Shemer! And what more?

MICAIAH

What more?

ASHOBAL

Good heaven, you surely ask no more?

NABOTH

I do. It's not enough.

JEZEBEL

Then name your price.

NABOTH

I cannot be buyer and seller both.

JEZEBEL

Then I will offer these: a bale of scarlet,
A camel-load of wool, woven or raw,
Three tent-rugs such as desert tribesmen weave,
Three desert-cushions made of coloured leather,
And one sealed roll of linen from the Nile,
The deckings of a house, in fact. With these,
Something to gladden dwellers in the house,
A score of honey, and a man-sized jar
Of olive oil, a measure of fine flour,
A pack of dates and seven porters' loads
Of matured wine; the feastings of a house.
With these, I offer treasures for your house:

Gums from Arabia to burn as perfumes,
A tusk of ivory two cubits long,
A bar of silver from the mines of Bakht,
A casket made of turkis filled with beryl,
A piece of gold, the size of a man's hand.

NABOTH

I want no ivory nor gold nor scarlet,
Nor silver bars nor trash nor vanity.

MICAIAH

Good Madam, might it not be wise to offer
Stock for his farm?

JEZEBEL

          Take horses, then, or oxen
To till your holding.

NABOTH

I will not take them, then.

MICAIAH

Would you not like them?

NABOTH

          No; I do without;
I need nor horse nor ass, nor cow nor camel.

JEZEBEL

What can I offer?

NABOTH

Sacrifice to the God of Israel.

JEZEBEL

I do not offer that.

NABOTH

          You are not one
To search unto the spirit, nor be single
Within your heart.　You are possessed by things;

Dead things, with stink and colour, brought in ships;
Your purples and the jewels for your hair,
Your ivory room, God save us! you being mortal,
Dwelling in ivory, while God himself
Lives in the wooden room darkened by wings.

MICAIAH

Yes, Naboth; but reserve this for the feast,
Where those who hear it will enjoy it more
Than we do here.

NABOTH

I do not speak to you.

JEZEBEL

No, Naboth, you are speaking to your Queen,
Who bids you to be silent, if you care
To keep whole bones. Come from him then, Micaiah.
Hear a last offer, Naboth: you are old,
Soon to become infirm, soon to bear pain,
And find it weariness to cross the room.
Might I not set provision for old age
Against your vineyard? Might I settle on you
A pension that would bring you quietness
And what age loves, respect and ease and state?
Might we not give you rank, as Elder, say,
With pay and servants fitting to the rank?
These things to be assured to you for life,
And after, to your son?

NABOTH

        I have no son.
My son was killed while fighting for King Ahab
In this last war. I will not sell my vineyard
For all the rank, for all the slaves and ease
In this realm that you make the gate of Hell.
God blot me from the record of the blest

If I give up my fathers' heritage,
If I commit into polluted hands,
Red with the blood of offerings to false gods,
The earth my father worked and worshipped in.
It is my vineyard and it shall be mine,
By God's red hand the King should be ashamed;
You too would be ashamed were you not shameless,
To tempt a poor man's soul with merchandise;
You, smeared with spice, painted, and dripping perfume,
A shameless woman, chaffering with a man,
And he, the King, a dallier with God's foes,
Conspiring thus to cheat me of my vineyard.
God puts a word into my mouth to say,
He makes my mouth to spit upon you both.
There is for you.   And there is for the King.
I spit upon you both and bid God curse you,
Curse you to ruin and to rottenness.
As here I curse you; him for making peace,
Where no peace is, and you, you insolent woman,
For being, like the King, a curse on Israel,
A bringer down into the pit of hell.

MICAIAH

You shall avoid the presence when you curse.

(*Exit with* NABOTH)

JEZEBEL

You heard the curses of this frantic man?

ASHOBAL *and* PHARMAS

Madam, we did.   We longed to silence him.

JEZEBEL

Rechab is captain of the guard to-day?

PHARMAS

Yes, Madam.

ASHOBAL

Rechab, with the Jezreel troop,
Mounts guard till night.

JEZEBEL

That will be well, Ashobal.
You know the ivory room that the King made?
You know that it was never planned nor used
For anything, save as an inmost shrine
For worshipping of God?

PHARMAS *and* ASHOBAL

We know it, Madam.

JEZEBEL

Here is Micaiah back. Has Naboth gone?

MICAIAH

Yes, Madam, to the rabble of his friends
Waiting his coming at the palace gate.
Now they are taking him triumphantly
Up to the feast, shouting, "He held his own
Against the royal tyrants." At the feast,
When they have drunken, they will speak worse evil.

JEZEBEL

You all remember what he uttered here?
How he misused the name of God, and cursed
The King and me?

MICAIAH, ASHOBAL *and* PHARMAS
(*Together*)

We do remember.

JEZEBEL

Wait, then, some minutes, till the feast be set,
Then summon up the chapter of the priests,
And Rechab with his troop of bodyguard.

Then march with priests and soldiers to the banquet.
Let the priests call for silence from the throng,
And in the silence do you three stand forth,
Bear witness against Naboth in these terms:
"Thou didst blaspheme God and the King!" repeat
The words he uttered, bear each other witness;
And if a further witness be required,
Say I, the Queen, will come to testify,
Who heard the words, yet spared the speaker of them,
So that the priests, whose cause it is, might judge.
Then call upon the priests to utter judgment
According to the laws of blasphemy.

MICAIAH, PHARMAS *and* ASHOBAL

We will obey your orders instantly.

(*They go out*)

JEZEBEL

Which brings the greater woe; to pass an evil,
Or break your Being's law to combat it?
The allotted sorrow ever has a gateway.

CURTAIN

ROSE-FLOWER

Nireus sailed; and a strange wind blew him to islands unseen
    before,
    Where the gods sat throned on the crags with peace on their
        marvellous faces,
Clouds and the smoke of fire, that glittered and changed, they
    wore;
    And unto them came the crying of all man's sorrowful races.

MOON-BLOSSOM

They cried to him as he passed, "You are seeking and you shall
    find,

Not in the way you hope, not in the way foreseen;
Out of horror of soul, ache, and anguish of mind,
  Out of the desert of all, shall come the leaf that is green."

ROSE-FLOWER

Then the wind blew on to an island where millet is ever in ear,
  And the horses that live in the sea come thronging in thousands to eat,
And the horses that live on the island will never let them come near,
  But they fight on the beaches forever with flashing and thunder of feet.

MOON-BLOSSOM

Then he sailed by invisible islands, he smelt the fruit on the trees,
  And heard the noise in the shipyards and the crowing of cocks unseen,
Then sheered from the roar of breakers and on over unknown seas,
  And ever he grieved for Paris, and thought of the beautiful Queen.

ROSE-FLOWER

Then he came to a sea of terror, where monsters rose from the sea,
  Things with the beaks of birds and arms like the suckers of vines:
Things like ghosts in the water coming motionlessly
  To tatter the flesh of men with teeth like the cactus-spines.

MOON-BLOSSOM

Over unending water ever he held his course,
  Birds that were curses followed, crying around and above:
"Nireus, broken by beauty, broken again by remorse,
  Goes to the breaking of death for killing his friend and love."

Rose-Flower

And ever he cursed himself for bringing them both to wreck,
  Helen and Paris, the lovely; and ever the waves seemed
    filled
With skull-bones hollow in death, that rose and peered on the
    deck:
  And he thought, "They are those from Troy whom I in my
    madness killed.

Moon-Blossom

"Had I refused, when they asked for my help to escape,
  Paris would still be alive, Troy, the city, would stand,
And all the killed of the war would be tilling the corn and the
    grape.
  Not ghosts with a curse in the air and torn bones strewing
    the land."

Rose-Flower

So he sailed; but at night in the dark when the lantern bubbled
    aloft,
  And men lay sleeping, when all save he were asleep,
And the ship slid on with a gurgle of water soft,
  He knew that the dead of Troy came with him over the deep.

Moon-Blossom

Out of the long-backed roller that slid from its crest of foam,
  Gibbered the bloodless dead, white faces with haggard eyes,
Pointing the bones of their hands at him who had forced them
    from home,
  Their curses came to his ears like little twittering cries.

Together

Whenever he moored at an island for water or food or rest,
  Soon those wraiths of the dead would rise and bid him begone,
To harry the resting gannet out of the roller's crest
  And carry the curse of his soul to the unknown, on and on.

Moon-Blossom

In the grey of morning
When the stars were paling,
Nireus sailing,
Saw land ahead.
An island shining
With city towers,
Where bells were ringing
And men singing.

Rose-Flower

As Nireus stepped ashore there
He stood staring,
For all men there
Were the dead of the war:
The Greeks and Trojans,
Beautiful and swift,
Killed in the trampled tamarisks
Beneath Troy town.

Moon-Blossom

Stars were in their hair,
Their brows were crowned with violets,
They stepped like stags,
Comrade with comrade.
They had forgotten
The mud and death,
The heat and flies
Of the plain of Troy.

Rose-Flower

There among them
Came a prince in scarlet,
With his hands stretched
In welcoming.

It was Paris, his friend,
Paris whom he killed
In the midnight raid
Beneath Troy wall.

Moon-Blossom

Paris cried,
"Nireus, my comrade,
Nireus, my beloved,
My friend of old!
Here we have forgiven
What my young man's folly bred,
We feast as friends
In the violet fields."

Rose-Flower

Then he led Nireus
To the hall of feasting.
There they feasted
In the violet fields.
Three summer days and nights,
It seemed, they feasted,
Each summer day and night
Was ten years long.

Together

Paris and the heroes
Cried to Nireus,
"We loved Helen,
When we were men.
Now we love her still
And we see her lonely,
Old, and haunted
By her lovers dead.

"Take to Helen
Gifts from her lovers,

In her old age find her
And give her these:
Beauty and peace
And our forgiveness,
And all our thanks
For what she was."

Moon-Blossom

As they ceased speaking
They faded from him,
The island faded,
Nireus was at sea.
He and his men
Were all grown old,
Thirty years
Had fallen on them.

Together

As old men failing
They came to Sparta;
All unavailing
Their coming was.
Helen was gone
And none knew whither,
To search for peace
Or to find release.

Over the seas
In lands and islands
Nireus sought her,
But could not find.
For the gods retire
When men desire,
Though it burn like fire
And make men blind.

THIRD ACT

Prophet

Come, you avenging Powers, who with swords
Smite at the bidding of your overlords;
Come, all you threatening things, who, with slant eyes,
Wait to snatch spirits in the mood unwise;
Come, eagle spirits, that do drink man's blood,
Hurry on smeared wings hither to your food:
I, who am Prophet, give you King and Queen.

(Enter Ashobal)

Ashobal

What are you raging for? Be silent, Prophet,
The King is coming hither.

Prophet

Tell him this:
"I am the herald of a mightier King,
Who bids me stand before this palace door
And cry a curse on Ahab and his wife.
Ahab, the dog, Ahab, the murderer,
And Jezebel the harlot murderess."

(Enter Ahab)

Ahab

So! Hast thou found me, O mine enemy?

Prophet

Yes, I have found thee, and before I lose thee
Will speak one word.   What hast thou done, thou devil,
On Naboth, that most upright man of God?

Ahab

An upright man is in God's hands, O Prophet.

A KING'S DAUGHTER251

PROPHET

True, he is in God's hands. Who sent him there?

AHAB

I know not, Prophet, but if he be there,
He will be much at peace.

PROPHET

You fiend of hell!
You, who have murdered Naboth, to exult
Over his corpse, still bleeding as it is.

AHAB

I have not murdered Naboth, nor do know
That he is dead, nor how, nor why. Explain.

PROPHET

You damned him to be stoned for blasphemy.

AHAB

I, do you say?

PROPHET

Yes, you; or if not you,
Your bloody-hearted hirelings and the priests.

AHAB

The priests alone can judge of blasphemy.
Which do you call my hirelings?

PROPHET

The accursed
Idolaters who follow on your Queen.

(*Enter* JEZEBEL)

JEZEBEL

I am the Queen. Where is the man who dares
Call those who follow me accurst?

PROPHET

Here, devil.

Here is the man who dare call you and them
Accurst as murderers of Naboth dead.

AHAB

You say that priests condemned him for blaspheming.

PROPHET

You stirred the priests to prosecuting him.

AHAB

No, not in any way soever, Prophet.

PROPHET

Then you, co-devil with him, did this thing.

JEZEBEL

Harken, old ruffian, and be warned by Naboth.
He cursed his God and King here in my presence,
Breaking the kingdom's laws of blasphemy.
I, who uphold this kingdom's laws gave order
That he should be arraigned for blasphemy.
Do I conclude that there are still some men
Who do their ruler's bidding in this kingdom?

AHAB

He was arraigned, condemned and stoned?

PROPHET

He was.

JEZEBEL

So perish all such breakers of the law.

PROPHET

Easily spoken words for King and Queen;
And easy laws for King and Queen to keep,

Living in purple in the ivory room;
And useful laws for killing enemies.
But there are other laws which do persist
After the enemies are killed. For Naboth
We left his body lying on its face,
And the wild dogs slink in and lick his blood;
And the bald birds that watch in heaven for deaths,
Settle, and wait until the dogs have done.
But . . . as those dogs and buzzards come to Naboth,
The dogs and kites of vengeance come to you.
I tell you this . . .
Since you have sold yourself thus to work evil,
I will bring evil on you, take away
All your posterity, and make your house
Like Jeroboam's house,
And like the accursed house, Baasha's house.
Those of your house that die within the city
The dogs shall eat, and those that die afield
The fowls of the air shall eat; and Jezebel . . .
Dogs shall eat Jezebel by the city wall.
Now royal rottenness in purple hedged,
I call a great cry from the Spirit of God.
Come all you dogs and vultures.
Come on your noiseless wings out of great Heaven,
Come upon padding footsteps stealthily.
Follow your victims in the hearts of men,
And by the ways of men, and take their blood
As they took his, as they took his, as they
Took his, upon the stones; blood, blood, that shrieks.

(The spirit passes out of him. He swoons)

AHAB

So, Jezebel, you see what you have done.

JEZEBEL

Would you have pardoned Naboth, had you heard him?

AHAB

No; but to give our enemies this handle
Against us, at this time, and for no reason.

JEZEBEL

The laws are plain: would you have pardoned him?

AHAB

I tell you, no.

Jezebel

Then what would you have done?

AHAB

Made him a mocking, or imprisoned him,
Or had him publicly displayed and shamed.

JEZEBEL

Why did you not then do as you have said?
I told you plainly of the need of action.
One of us rulers had to play the King
And check this rebel.   Since you did not, I did.
And he is checked forever, and his friends
Daunted: so daunted that you have the chance
Now, to take hold and be indeed the King
And rule according to your royal will,
Not as the frenzy of a rebel bids.

AHAB

This thing that you have done has ruined all
The little chance I had of governing.
You bring me to the pitch of having to choose
Between your fancies and the people's will.
Perhaps it is too late to remedy
The evil that must follow from your folly.
Naboth is dead: this prophet shows our future;
If there be any future left for us.

Do not now answer me; I must debate this
Within myself. You may have ruined me,
But that or no, you have been mad, by Heaven.

(*Exit* AHAB)

JEZEBEL

How blest to be a prophet, who forever
Does but condemn another man's endeavour.
How blest, not to decide, nor be, nor do,
But help the many to condemn the few.

(*Enter* JORAM)

Joram, my son, do you come to comfort your mother?

JORAM

No, mother, I do not. I come to look for my father.

JEZEBEL

If you are looking for the King, this is the King.

JORAM

What is this body, Madam? The prophet? Is he dead?

JEZEBEL

Only swooned from cursing your father and mother.

JORAM

Mother, you are talking very strangely.

JEZEBEL

I have been mad, by Heaven. Why, Joram, you come to
tell your father so; do you not, boy?

JORAM

I do not know how to answer you.

JEZEBEL

You reckon me a curse upon this country?

JORAM

As my father's officer I have to report what the citizens feel.

JEZEBEL

You feel it with them.

JORAM

Whatever I feel I can restrain; but since you insist, I say that it is hard that my father should be ruined by your Syrian policy and gods and self.

JEZEBEL

You are half Syrian.

JORAM

Through you, I was. But in this last war, while I lay wounded, a Syrian trooper kicked me and spurred me in the face. That took my last drop of Syrian blood; your blood. There is nothing Syrian in me now. But I mean to pay the Syrians for that kicking and spurring when they lie wounded. You have made father mild and Ahaziah like yourself; but after them perhaps I shall be King; perhaps sooner.

JEZEBEL

You are leagued with your father's enemies. And do you think that they will make you the King?

JORAM

It is not a question of what I think, but of the needs of this land.

JEZEBEL

When the mob comes to sack the palace, there is always some prince to open the door.

JORAM

If I ever am the King, the Syrians will see.

JEZEBEL

May it be long before you become King.

JORAM

Your killing Naboth may make it very long. But I am not here to talk with you, but with the King.

JEZEBEL

As I told you, this is the King, here on the ground.

(*Enter* AHAB)

JORAM

Save you, O King, I bring a message from the Council.

AHAB

What is it?

JORAM

Something that would be better said by Ahaziah than myself.

AHAB

Let me hear it.

JORAM

If I did not bring it as a message, it would be my duty as your officer to bring it as a report.

JEZEBEL

The Council sends word by your son that you, the King, should banish the Queen.

JORAM

Madam, do not add to the pain of my mission. The Council is composed of manly and godly men, the best of our country, whose wills are worth the weighing. They bid me say, sir, this, that they deplore that such a King should have for counsellor one who brings peace with Syria, and the death of an upright man whom they esteemed.

AHAB

By this counsellor they mean your mother, the Queen?

JORAM

Sir, you are ever wise and they ever respectful. They feel that a foreign influence is not for your people's good, nor for justice in your people's causes.

JEZEBEL

My son, speak openly, for the people's good.

AHAB

What do they demand?

JORAM

They bid me say, Sir, that they cannot doubt that you would care only for your people's good, were it made apparent.

JEZEBEL

Make it apparent.

JORAM

Sire, I would that the prince, my brother, might have had this task.

JEZEBEL

I, too, wish that, my son. Is not banishment enough, then? Do they ask for my death?

JORAM

Sir, those are their feelings.

AHAB

They hate my Queen and wish her gone?

JORAM

Sir, truth cannot be hidden from you.

AHAB

And if I ignore their feelings, or crush their mutterings?

JORAM

Sir, they think you too great a man, for either way.

AHAB

But if they err, and I do?

JORAM

You would not.

AHAB

If I did, what then?

JORAM

Your Majesty has too good a memory.

AHAB

What do you mean by that, boy?

JORAM

Sir, your father only came to the crown because a former King ignored men's feelings. King Nadab ignored his subjects' feelings. What happened to him? King Elah did. What happened to him? King Zimri did. What happened to him? Men now living saw all these Kings; and what came to them? The crown is granted on certain terms, according with the Life of this Race. My father, I beseech you, think what this Race asks.

AHAB

I never cease to think it. Leave us.

(*Exit* JORAM)

You heard what he said?

JEZEBEL

Yes.

AHAB

They want me to put you aside.

JEZEBEL

Yes, Ahab.

AHAB

What urged you to prosecute Naboth at such a time?

JEZEBEL

Someone had to act.

AHAB

You acted fatally.

JEZEBEL

I was myself, Ahab: a princess of Sidon; your Queen.

AHAB

This is not Sidon, but Shemer.

JEZEBEL

I will not plead for your forgiveness, then.
Dismiss me from your council and your court
And let me be; the hated foreign woman
Who tried and failed.   I will be nothing here.
After these years of hatred it will be
Peace to be nothing.   When my son returns,
(The captain, Ahaziah) send him hence.
I sent for him to help me govern here.
Since I am nothing now, he must not stay.
But now that I am nothing, I say this:
That you must be upon your guard, King Ahab.
More; you must play the King, and being King,
Strike down this prophet and his friend, Lord Jehu,
For they are linked together against peace.

AHAB

What proofs have you?

JEZEBEL

                A woman has no proofs,
Only an instinct fortified by love
Stronger than any proof.

AHAB

                And I have knowledge.
Jehu has been my captain of the horse,

My comrade in the field, my counsellor,
My soldier, who has shed his blood for me
In five campaigns, in many years of war.
This prophet is indeed the enemy
Of much that I have planned, but as for Jehu,
I know him, and I know that you have wronged him
And speak from bitterness.

JEZEBEL

Ahab, beware.

By all our lives together, you beware
Of Jehu and this man.

AHAB

Had I been ware of you, Queen Jezebel,
Many years sooner, I had had no need
To be aware of any of my subjects.
I cannot longer countenance your dealings.
They neither suit my people nor the time. Therefore
I do dismiss you from your royalty,
From queenship and command and counselling,
From all authority in Shemer here.
This shall be straightway published as my will.

PROPHET

The messenger that spoke through me has gone,
And I am cold and broken as with blows,
But yet I hear—can you not hear—do you?

AHAB

What should we hear, old ruffian from the desert?

PROPHET

The wings descending and the footsteps coming.
The vultures and the dogs coming for blood.
Listen. The vultures settle in the court,

And there are footsteps coming up the stair,
The footsteps of the dogs that come for blood;
For blood is coming upon this house, and I
Have told you that it comes; I am its herald.
(*Enter* JEHU *from in front, carrying armour. He comes on,
stands motionless, then flings down a helmet; then, after a
pause, a corselet; then, after a pause, a sword. ZAKKUR
stands behind him.*)

AHAB

What does your coming with these weapons mean?
Whose weapons are they? What has happened, Jehu?
Is it some challenge? Speak.

JEZEBEL

    I know that sword.
It's Ahaziah's sword. My son is dead?

(JEHU *nods*)

AHAB

What? Ahaziah dead? How did he die?

JEHU

While he was riding here, he made a halt,
To rest his horses, at the inn at Springs;
And leaning on the lattice, looking out,
He fell out of the upper balcony,
And died soon after, broken by the fall.
Here is the witness, who will tell you how.

AHAB

Speak then, and tell the tale. How could he fall?

ZAKKUR

By treachery, by Syrian treachery. Lord, when our Queen
commanded the Prince to return here, she sent her orders by a
Syrian of the court.

JEZEBEL

I did, by Malik.

ZAKKUR

Malik was in the pay of the King of Syria.

JEZEBEL

That is false. That lie has been exposed many times over.

ZAKKUR

Madam, alas, it is now proven, by Malik's confession.

AHAB

Who are you, who speak?

ZAKKUR

A lieutenant in our late Prince's troop, my lord.

AHAB

Go on, then, about Malik.

ZAKKUR

Before delivering his orders to our late Prince, he showed them to the Syrian officers in the garrison at Ramoth. They saw a chance of intercepting our Prince upon his way. They bribed Malik to lead the Prince, so as to halt at the inn at Springs. They did not wish to set upon him, because they expected the troop to be with the Prince. They sawed through the beams of the balcony of the inn, so that when he set foot upon it, the floor should give way. The Prince did not bring his troop with him, but set out with myself, his galloper, and Malik. He halted at the inn, at Malik's persuasion, much against his will, for he wished to be here. Then all happened as his murderers the Syrians had devised. He went upon the balcony, it fell, and he died from it.

After he had died, my lord, Malik urged us to come away, which I and my colleague would not, without examination. When we found that the beams had been sawn, remembering

Malik's Syrian birth and his suspicious wishes, first to halt
there, then to come away, we taxed him with the crime and he
confessed, and was secured.

The galloper waits at the inn for an escort for the body and
the prisoner. It was decided that I should ride here at once
with the news.

JEZEBEL

Before he died, did he say anything?

ZAKKUR

Yes, Madam; he muttered about the gods, and about you.

JEZEBEL

What did he say?

ZAKKUR

That we were to tell you that this was the gods' reward for
peace with Syria.

JEZEBEL

Since he is dead, wisdom and peace are dead!

(*She goes out*)

AHAB

God, thou hast faced me with my sin this day.
My son, who was to follow me as King,
Killed by a Syrian plot, by treachery.
Killed, coming home to help me in my sorrows.

PROPHET

Killed by your treachery, that made the peace
With Syria, against God's ordinance.

JEHU

Nothing that has been done by Syria
Against this land, can rank beside this deed;
The loss of such a prince by such a crime

Will rouse this country, lord. You will keep peace
By your great policy, but through your people
A mighty cry for vengeance will arise.

Ahab

And not unheeded, Jehu. Listen, all.
This was his sword. He was to be the King
After my death, fulfilling all my dreams.
See, you, and you, and you, I take the sword
And draw it out and swear upon its hilt
To take a vengeance on the murderers
Who brought him to his death.

Jehu

                   Well sworn, O King!

Prophet

Surely the Spirit of God is working in you!

Ahab

Wait yet, O Prophet; though my heart is sick
At having trusted in my enemies
And been ill-paid, I will ask help from God;
Counsel and help in any act of justice.
Go, gather me the prophets, let them seek
Illumination, then bring word to me
Whether the spirit do approve a war.
I will go seek for guidance, though my heart
Seeks less for guidance now than for release.

Jehu

Lord, all true hearts commiserate your grief.

Ahab

Thank you, good Jehu.
            (*Exit* Ahab)

ZAKKUR

Well, he took the story.

JEHU

Yes, as I knew he would. The score's one each.
He has won Naboth, I have Ahaziah.

PROPHET

Was not the story true?

JEHU

                                The Prince is dead,
So much is true; and in an hour from now
We can be marching hence with Ahab's self,
If all your prophets will but prophesy.
I want him killed in war, outside the city.
Go, bid the prophets prophesy for war.

                    (*Exit* PROPHET, *with* ZAKKUR)

JEHU

So, Ahaziah, you were rude to me.
Princes should not be rude to rising men,
For men may rise. You will be rude no more.
I have been rude to you, my Ahaziah.
I kicked the lips that once were rude to me.
My foot is on your heart's blood, Ahaziah.

CURTAIN

MOON-BLOSSOM

Full of years and wealth and evil, Menelaus died in Sparta,
    And Queen Helen at his bedside stood and looked upon him
        dead,
He who once had bought her beauty, to be bride for him, by
    barter,

He whom she had loathed and fled from, now lay silenced
   on the bed.

Rose-Flower

Bitter thoughts were in her as she looked upon his meanness,
   Thoughts of Paris in his beauty when their love was at its
     height,
Paris in his morning, and the King in his uncleanness,
   And this dead mean thing, her master, and the winner of the
     fight.

Together

All was silent in the palace of the King,
Save the soft-foot watchers whispering;
   All was dark, save in the porch
   The wind-blown fire of a torch,
And the sentries still as in a stound,
With their spear-heads drooped upon the ground.

Rose-Flower

Then she thought: "These two men had me, and a myriad men
   have sickened
   To a fever of a love for me who saw me passing by:
When they saw me, all their eyes grew bright, and all their
   pulses quickened,
   And to win me or to keep me they went up to Troy to die.

Moon-Blossom

"Now the earthly moon, my beauty, and the rose, my youth,
   have dwindled,
   I am old, my hair is grey, and none remembers
What a fire in men's hearts Queen Helen kindled
   Ere the fire in Queen Helen turned to embers."

Together

All was silent in the palace of the King,
Save the wind-blown torch-flame guttering,

And a moth that came
  Beating with his wings about the flame,
And the sentries drawing breath,
With their spear-heads drooped saluting death.

Moon-Blossom

Then she said: "The gods conspired to give gifts of beauty to
    me,
And the beauty gave the gift of death to all who came to woo
    me;
  Now of all the men who loved me, none remain,
And of both the men who had me neither knew me—
  Surely all my past was evil, for its fruit is bitter pain.

Rose-Flower

"I will go to some lone island where I am not made a story,
  Where my beauty made no widow, nor no orphan wanting
    bread;
Where no human sorrow suffers the disaster of my glory,
  And my eyes may lose the vision of the hauntings of the dead.

Moon-Blossom

"Day and night the dead men haunt me, whom the madness
    of my caring
  Brought from home and wives and children to be bones upon
    the plain;
All the panther-like for beauty, all the lion-like for daring,
  And they lie among the bindweed now, uncovered by the
    rain."

Together

All was silent in the palace of the King,
Save the soft-foot watchers whispering;
  All was dark, save in the porch
  The wind-blown fire of a torch,
And the sentries still as in a stound
With their spear-heads drooped upon the ground.

Then she rose, and cloaked her face, and hurried swiftly from
    the city,
    And to sea, away from Hellas, but she dared not show her
        face,
For the women and the orphans would have killed her without
    pity;
    She had sown her crop of death too far; she found no resting-
        place.

But in inns where people gathered in the evenings after labour,
    Where the shepherd's pipe or viol stirred the blind man to
        his verse,
Till the hearers swayed and trembled and the rough man
    touched his neighbour,
    They would talk of Troy with sadness, but of Helen with a
        curse.

Moon-Blossom

After long years, when Helen was riding by night
    In storm, in the Ida forest, alone, not knowing the road,
She saw a light in the blackness; she turned to the light,
    She came to the fort on the crag, the panther-women's abode.

Rose-Flower

Hearing her horse's stamp, they brought her into the yard,
    Those women fierce from the killing of lion or boar or man;
They came with their torches round her, they stared at her
    hard,
    They knew her for Helen the Queen from whom their sorrows
        began.

For years they had longed for her coming, to have her to kill,
    Her beauty a throat for their knives, her body a prey—
Helen, who ruined their lovers, the root of their ill—
    She said: "I am Helen. Avenge yourselves on me. You
    may."

Moon-Blossom

Still they stared at her there in the torchlight; then one of them
    said:
   "God used you to bring things to be; evil things to our city,
Evil things to yourself, for your face declares you have paid;
    You have come to the truth like ourselves; we take not
      vengeance, but pity."
Then they welcomed her into their hold, and when morning
    broke clear,
   They rode with her down to the ruins of what had been Troy;
There they left her alone in the wreck of the thing over-dear
    That the gods cannot grant to mankind, but unite to destroy.

FOURTH ACT

Jezebel

I shall not look upon my son again!
How many million mothers must have felt
As I, with a dead child.   How many lives
Have been made lightless thus.
For no child ever dies without the breaking
Of someone's heart.
And yet the world goes on.
I shall go on, perhaps for many years,
And in my heart's most secret corridor
Will be a shrine, where I shall watch my son,
Lonely as Helen in her tower at Troy
When Paris had been killed.
Would I had been beside him when he fell,
And fallen with him to the pit of death!
Better die so, not mangled in the war,
A young man, beautiful in youth, as thou wert;

Not troubled yet by life; not yet a King;
Thou hast been only young and now art dead.
With all life's faults, I want you back in life,
Not dead, my son, beyond my touch and speech,
But here, moving and speaking, being mine.
My help and stay and wisdom and assuagement
As in the past. You, who gave no farewell,
Speak to me from the grave, O lovely son.

(There is a sighing)

Was that an answer from the dead, or birds
Flying away before the winter comes?
My son, if you are there, speak to my spirit.

(There is a sighing)

What message do you bring; that you are here,
What do you come to tell me?

THE VOICE

Death.

JEZEBEL

What?

THE VOICE

Death.

JEZEBEL

Whose death? Mine? Or your father's? Or the kingdom's?
My son's soul was within this room and speaking.
O speak again, say something, give me proof
That you are linked still by dear love to me.
Hark! Hush!
No. There was no voice speaking; nor will be.

(AHAZIAH appears)

My boy! My son!

AHAZIAH

Mother!

JEZEBEL

My child! My dear!

AHAZIAH

Listen. I cannot say it all. The flowers
Speak truth. You all are coming.

JEZEBEL

             Then, beloved,
We shall soon meet again, and part no more.

AHAZIAH

Mother, I struggle back to tell you this:
It is most hard to come, most hard to speak.
You must with all your power strive to cut
These nets.

JEZEBEL

What are these nets?

AHAZIAH

           The nets of death,
That are all round you like a hunter's toils.

JEZEBEL

Do you mean civil war? Or war with Syria?

AHAZIAH

That is not what I mean; but someone near you.
Someone about you has most deadly hands,
A hangman's hands; and you must break his hands.

JEZEBEL

Who is it, that is deadly? Is it Joram?

AHAZIAH

I cannot speak his name, but, mother, hark:
He murdered me; I never saw his face;
He killed me at the inn.

JEZEBEL

Jehu, you mean?

AHAZIAH

The man forever looking at the throat,
Whose fingers twitch; a red-eyed man it is,
I cannot speak the name.

JEZEBEL

O it is Jehu!
And Jehu murdered you?

AHAZIAH

There's danger, mother;
Avoid the nets. I cannot make you see them.

JEZEBEL

Jehu is spreading nets of treachery?

AHAZIAH

The flowers speak truth; the flowers and the rod,
The riding rod.

(*He goes*)

JEZEBEL

O speak! O my dear son,
How can I help, I being queen no longer,
But banished and condemned? What can I do?
And what is this of riding rods and flowers?

(*There is a sighing*)

My son is gone into the night of Death,
And Jehu murdered him in ways unknown.
Would I could prove the crime!

(*Enter* MICAIAH)

MICAIAH

Madam, a rider from the inn at Springs

Has brought these flowers, gathered by the prince
Your son, now dead.

JEZEBEL

The flowers that speak truth!
Was there no other relic but the flowers?

MICAIAH

Yes, Madam, this: a staff or riding rod,
Left on the flowers, so the rider said.

JEZEBEL

A riding rod! And do you know the rod?

MICAIAH

Madam, I do. It is Lord Jehu's staff.

JEZEBEL

What brought it to the inn at Springs, Micaiah?

MICAIAH

I do not know. The rider found it there.

JEZEBEL

Where is the rider who delivered these?

MICAIAH

Gone, Madam; he preferred not to be known.

JEZEBEL

I see you have suspicions; let me know them.

MICAIAH

Madam, this staff was in Lord Jehu's hand
This morning, when I saw him here at court.

JEZEBEL

That, or one like it? Could you swear to that?

MICAIAH

He held this staff.   He stopped me in the square
About a warrant, and I noticed it.
This little scratch is unmistakable.

JEZEBEL

And what can you conclude from this, Micaiah?

MICAIAH

That the Lord Jehu hurried to the Springs,
After I saw him, and then hurried back.

JEZEBEL

What duty could have taken him to Springs?

MICAIAH

Madam, he had no duty there.   I asked.

JEZEBEL

Might not a messenger have gone from him
Bearing his staff?

MICAIAH

Madam, he went himself.
The warden at the west gate saw him start
In that direction, and return from thence
Three hours later.   He was back by noon.

JEZEBEL

So that he would have been at Springs, perhaps,
Before Prince Ahaziah halted there?

MICAIAH

Perhaps.

JEZEBEL

Yet not perhaps; he would have been there,
He must have been there at the very time.

MICAIAH

Madam, I dare not utter thoughts like these.

JEZEBEL

Yet Jehu could not know that he was coming
Home from the frontier, or would pass by Springs.

MICAIAH

So please you, Madam, but the fact was known
Publicly in the city everywhere.
The knowledge was abroad, I know not how.
You are beset by watchers, and by traitors.

JEZEBEL

And murderers and friends of murderers.
Jehu waylaid my son and murdered him.
By these poor relics sacred with his blood
I will denounce him to the King myself,
Or lay him dead before me with my hands.

(She gathers the relics)

MICAIAH

Lie there, sad relics of a glorious youth.

ZIKRI *(entering)*

Make ready for the utterance of the Prophet!

KALLAI

Bow down before the Prophet, bringer of truth!

(Enter the PROPHET)

PROPHET

I am bringer of Truth out of the hidden,
I am finder of ways where footing is sure,
I am sword and shield against things forbidden,
I am brightness to guide, healing to cure;
Mine are the words that endure.

I, now, about to declare as the Spirit orders,
Cry, let women avoid, let children hide,
Let none but spearmen be here, the city's warders.
I speak, out of the Truth, words that abide,
Men only may hear what might of men must decide.
(JEZEBEL *veils and goes. Enter* JORAM, *then* JEHU, *then* AHAB,
   preceded by SPEARMEN)

AHAB

Now that the revelation is vouchsafed,
Stand, all, before this Prophet, who has seen
Light in the darkness that has blinded us.

PROPHET

Harken, O King, to revelation's self.
The spirit says, "Go up against the Syrians;
At Ramoth-Gilead you shall conquer them."
See here these horns of iron that I wear.
The spirit says, "With these horns shalt thou push
The Syrians, until they be consumed."

JEHU

Good messages, good omens, good foretellings.

AHAB

May they prove good.

JORAM

The spirit filled the prophets with a glory
Marvellous to watch and hear: they spoke as one.

MICAIAH

Not quite as one, Prince Joram and my King.
One was not filled with spirit.

AHAB

Who is this?

Micaiah

I am Micaiah, Lord, who have been counted
A seer, too, at times.

Ahab

             O it is you!
Honest Micaiah, who must speak the truth.
I hate this man; he prophesies not good
But evil of me.

Jehu

These fellows are too ready with their evil.

Pharmas (*To* Micaiah)

See now, the prophets foretell victory,
With one mouth; say the same; cry victory.

Micaiah

As the Lord lives I'll speak what the Lord says.

Ahab

Micaiah, shall we go to Ramoth-Gilead
To battle, or forbear?

Micaiah

           Go, Lord, and prosper,
The Lord shall make it yours.

Ahab

            How many times
Shall I adjure you that you speak the truth
Speak nothing but the truth.

Joram

I'd have a way to make him speak the truth.
Two troopers with a pair of stirrup leathers
To teach his obstinate jaw some reverence.

AHAB

Peace, Joram; let him speak.

MICAIAH

Sir, I will speak.
In dreams, last night, in the dark night, ere cocks crowed,
I saw a downland empty to the sky.

JORAM

That is the way these fellows use to talk;
They'd talk another way, had I my will.

MICAIAH

And suddenly I saw all Israel
Scattered upon that downland frantically,
Like sheep without a shepherd.   The Lord said:
"These have no master now; let them go home."

AHAB

And how do you interpret this your dream?

MICAIAH

That if you go this warfare, you, the master
Of Israel, will die.

AHAB

How die?

MICAIAH

I do not know.

JEHU

You mean in battle?

MICAIAH

By violence.

JORAM

That means in battle, surely.

MICAIAH

Not necessarily.

JEHU

How else, then, man?

MICAIAH

I do not know.   Perhaps by treachery.

JEHU

We will protect the King from treachery.

JORAM (*To* MICAIAH)

Except such treachery as men like you
Think in their hearts and utter in big words,
Trying to wreck the State.

AHAB

                    Did I not say
That he would utter evil about me?

JORAM

These fellows need a bit within their jaws.

MICAIAH

My prince, no bit can stop the telling truth.

PROPHET

What do you know of truth, idolater?

MICAIAH

Nothing.   I know that certain things are true.

JEHU

Fine talk, to keep the army lingering.

AHAB

Have you some other vision to reveal?

MICAIAH

A sort of vision.

PROPHET

Ay, a sort of vision.
There is one way of vision, only one,
Vouchsafed to men, you false one, with false gods.

AHAB

What is this vision?   Will it lighten me?

MICAIAH

It is of you and of the prophet tribe.

PROPHET

Some blasphemy.   Take heed to what he says.

MICAIAH

In the dark night I saw this other thing:
I saw the Lord in heaven on his throne,
With all the host of heaven standing by him.
He said, "Who shall persuade King Ahab to go up
And die at Ramoth-Gilead?"   They discussed it.
At last a spirit said, "I will persuade him."
The Lord said, "How?"
The spirit said, "I will go forth and be
A lying spirit in his prophets' mouths."
And the Lord said, "Thou shalt.   Go forth and do so."
Behold the Lord hath put a lying spirit
Into thy prophets' mouths, and spoken evil
Not good to you.

PROPHET

You think God's truth has passed from me to you.
When did it pass, and how?

MICAIAH

You will know that

When you shall go into an inner chamber
To hide yourself.

AHAB

Carry this fellow to the Governor,
And have him into prison in the dark,
And let his bread and drink be bitterness
Until I come in peace.

MICAIAH

If you return at all
In peace, the spirit has not spoken by me.
Hearken, O people, every one of you.

AHAB

Have him away.

MICAIAH

Which story is the likelier to be true,
Mine, which when told brings prison, or this fellow's
Which earns the King's reward?   The truth is dangerous.

JORAM

You'll find this dangerous.   Away with him!
(*He is dragged out.*)

JEHU

That shows how close your enemies can come.
Even to your very court.

JORAM

He should be silenced.

AHAB

He is a gallant fellow, without judgment.
But he presumes too much, he and his dreams.

PROPHET (*Crying aloud*)

O King, a vision is vouchsafed to me!
I see! I see! Hearken to what I see.

I see a red bull trampling down God's foes;
He neezes fire and all his fell is fire;
His shoulder is a mountain rough with forest;
His eye the wrath of God; he stamps the cities.
Go up against the Syrians, like this bull.

JORAM

There is the voice of God.

JEHU

Ay, truly, Prince.

AHAB

Since God declares that we should make this war,
Which we, as men, have shrunk from hitherto,
Although provoked by countless insolence,
Now hearken to the utterance of the crown.

(*Enter* JEZEBEL)

JEZEBEL

Ay, hearken to the utterance of the crown.
You are all come to hear a war declared.
Now, I, the crown, declare it unto you.
I declare war upon our enemies.
They are all present, standing in this place,
Waiting the execution of our sword.

(*To* PROPHET)

This man, the madman from the desert, first,
Who rages like a desert-storm, that kills
With sand, burning hot sand, pitiless sand.

(*To* JORAM)

This next, the hater of his house, our son,
Who, for a wound that pains him would be glad
That thousand others should be sick with wounds.

(*To* JEHU)

Then, next, this other man, not mad, not sick,

Not even suspected; honoured, trusted, loved.
This man, the rider to the inn at Springs,
For secret evil.   Hark! This man, King Ahab,
Murdered our son and plots to murder you.
Seize him, King Ahab, ere it be too late.

AHAB

Murdered our son?   But this is childishness.

JEZEBEL

No, I bring proof; the rod, the rod he holds,
Was found at Springs, to prove that he was there.

JEHU

This rod, good Madam?

JEZEBEL

Even that very rod.

AHAB

Who found it at the Springs?   Who brought it here?

JEZEBEL

A rider, lord, who gave it to Micaiah.

JORAM

What rider?

AHAB

Yes, what rider, can you tell?

JEZEBEL

One who would not be known, Micaiah said.

AHAB

Micaiah!   He?

JORAM

The man imprisoned here.

Jehu

My lord, I grieve less at this ill suspicion
Than at the sad disaster which has caused it.

Jezebel

You killed my son most foully at the inn;
You were seen riding thither before noon,
And left your rod there while you did the deed,
Upon these flowers which my son had gathered;
These desert flowers.

Jehu

My lord and King, I can most clearly prove
That I was at my quarters all the morning.
This rod I missed this morning from my quarters
And found it here on entering but now.
Prince Joram saw me find it as I entered.

Joram

That is most true; I did.
Mother, you should not be here; come away.

Jezebel

My Lord, my King, my husband, listen to me.
You know me, whether I am mad or no.
I am not mad; but Ahaziah's spirit
Came to me here, stood where his murderer stands,
Less than an hour ago, denouncing him,
His murderer, and traitor to yourself.
I, knowing this, see to the soul of things,
And cry, if you be man, attack this traitor,
Tear out his wicked plottings and destroy him.

Ahab

Let the Queen's women come. I hear your charges
Brought with more passion than with evidence.

These are our friends, our proven soldier, Jehu,
Our son, and this, the prophet of the spirit,
Not what you think.   See, here your women come.
Tend the Queen's majesty to her apartments.

JEZEBEL

You think me mad, my inmost wisdom, mad.
For the last time, for Ahaziah's sake,
For your sake, for the kingdom, for the crown,
And for the sake of God who gives the crown,
Believe what I have said against this Jehu.

AHAB

I grieve that anyone should bring such charges.
That you should bring them is an anguish to me.
Go with your women hence, and try to rest.

JEZEBEL

Prince Joram, will you give me your support?
Thank you, my son.
               Since no one will believe,
I, here, the Queen, must act alone.   I will.
(*She snatches* JORAM'S *knife and tries to kill* JEHU)
Die, murderer of my son!

JORAM (*Catching her*)
            I thought you'd try it.
But I was ready for you.   Come now, mother,
You must go rest.   Come help her there, you women.
            (JEZEBEL *is helped off*)
It is my brother's death that makes her thus.

AHAB

It shakes us all.   You understand, Duke Jehu,
The cause of this, without my saying more.

JEHU

My lord, I understand.
But yet suggest some trial or enquiry
Into my dealings.

AHAB

Do not think of it.
For these unhappy things which bruise men's hearts
Tear women's hearts across. Let us proceed.
I declare war against the Syrians
For breach of treaty. We will march at once.

JORAM

Though wounded, I will march, for I'll repay
The Syrians what I owe. Come, prophet, spread
The news throughout the city.

PROPHET

I will declare God's wrath against His enemies.

(JORAM *and* PROPHET *go*)

AHAB

Stay, Jehu, yet. You heard Micaiah's dream.
That was an evil omen for our war.

JEHU

I do not think so. Why, what was the dream?
That there should seem to be no King to-day.
Was not that it? The meaning is apparent:
That you should wear disguise.

AHAB

Ha! Well suggested.

JEHU

It is a wise precaution at the least.
Some traitor may be plotting to destroy you,

Some Syrian assassin may be here.
So take Micaiah's hint and wear no purple.

AHAB

A good interpretation. I accept it
So. I will march disguised.

JEHU

Much better so.

AHAB

Micaiah did interpret for my death.

JEHU

These thinkers are the enemies of war
Because they are afraid. He wished to scare you.
Let me unclasp the buckle of your cloak.
Much wiser give no target to these archers;
Wear the plain armour of a charioteer.

AHAB

I will, Duke Jehu. Lie you there, my purple,
Till I return to-night, with victory.
At sunset every night the Queen and I
Go through the citron gardens to the kennels,
To feed our Hittite wolf-hounds with raw flesh.
To-night when we go to feed them, we will go
As conquerers of Syria, through the city.

(*Exit* AHAB)

JEHU

Right, my good Lord. Yes, you shall be disguised;
But this bright bird within the quiver here
Will pierce through your disguise before to-night,
And you shall feed the wolf-hounds, never fear;
So shall your Queen, with royal flesh and raw.

(*He puts on the King's purple*)

Oh, out in the desert, my spear and my bow
　　Will win me whatever I need;
The wine and the oil that another did grow
　　And the horse that another did breed.
So away for the desert. . . .

Ay, I have trotted in your bodyguard
Too long, by God!

CURTAIN

ROSE-FLOWER

Queen Helen left those women of the wood,
　　She clambered from her horse and stood again
Even on the very hill where Troy had stood,
　　Where tamarisk shrubs and broom-sprigs and wild grain
　　Sprouted from bronze and rib-bones of men slain.

There was the palace where her love had been;
　　Stones blackened by the fire and misplace't
　　By roots of vines that fed upon the paste
Of all the pride where she had lived a queen.

Troy was no more than weeds and fire-flaked stone,
　　But still the straits ran roaring to the south,
And still the never quiet winds were blown
　　With scent of meadow-sweet from Simois' mouth.

MOON-BLOSSOM

Yet now no Greeks were moving on the beaches,
　　No galleys of the Greeks came oaring in,
　　Nor did lancer scouts or parties ride the whin,
Bringing in or checking convoys from the river's upper reaches
　　Where the forest pines begin.

And the forges were all gone, and all the fires

Of the camps and burnings of the dead;
And the grinding of the bronze-shod chariot tyres
                    Rang no more.
                    Both in city and on shore
There were no more shouted orders, clash of arms or marchers'
    tread.

ROSE-FLOWER

All was manless now, uncared for; both the streams had left
    their courses,
    There was marsh where corn had grown of old; and there,
    where Paris lay,
Was an apple tree with fruit which fed the now wild Trojan
    horses,
    That with bright teeth bit each other;
    Earth made Greek and Trojan brother,
All the passion that had raged there now was dead and gone
    away.

MOON-BLOSSOM

Then she cried, "I caused the quarrel that brought death along
    these beaches,
    I alone made Troy this ruin, I alone, from haste of youth,
From a woman's bent, that listens to a lie, if it beseeches;
    Now I stand here old and friendless, having nothing but the
    truth."

ROSE-FLOWER

There she stopped, for there before her, in the ruins, stood a
    stranger;
    "This is changed indeed," he told her, "since I stood here
    once before:
Then it flamed all red to heaven and it rang with death and
    danger,
    And I stood here with noble Agamemnon
    In the thunder of the ending of the war."

Moon-Blossom

Something in the old man's bearing made her start and catch
    her breath.
    "You are Nireus, friend," she answered.
      "You are he who brought me here
    When my life and love were dear:
Then I came to life and loving, now I come to grief and death.

"There is no small grass, in plain or water,
    But grows from the body of one killed
By the deadly love of me, who am Helen, Leda's daughter:
    All the young and swift and lovely, all the quick of heart are
      stilled;
I was cause of their going to the slaughter.

"Daylong and nightlong their shadows pursue me with evil,
    Haunting my thought in the day, killing my rest in the night;
Now they have drawn me here; their multitudinous devil
    Bids me die where I sinned.
    I hear their cry in the wind,
I see their eyes in the light."

Rose-Flower

Nireus answered, "Ah, not thus, not so, Queen Helen, surely,
    Are those who died for love of you, to win you or to keep!
If they gave their lives, they gave them, as a man gives frankly,
      purely,
    Without question, comment or complaint,
    The strong heart equal with the faint,
All content to see your beauty and to tread hard ways to sleep.

"Now they know that your beauty made them splendid,
    Splendid to the death; for I have seen,
Seen and talked, beloved Helen, with the souls of those who
    ended

In the ruins of this city that has been.
And they praise your name, they count you still their Queen.

"Now come with me, for the ship waits to receive you,
   The wind is fair for Symé; let us start.
Here, where long ago I lost you, I retrieve you;
   Let us leave this town of broken heart
For the peace of Symé harbour and the mirth of Symé mart,
     And the calm of knowing sorrow at an end
     And the quiet of the memory of a friend."

Together

Then they sailed for Symé Island, and the gods were with their
    going,
   For their beauty came upon them both, with youth and
   strength and peace;
Now they rule and live forever in a spring forever blowing
   High in Symé where the sun is bright and skylarks never cease.

FIFTH ACT

Rose-Flower

There is no rider, coming from the army,
In sight yet, Madam.   Shall we play again?
        (*No answer*)

Moon-Blossom

Come to the window.   There.   What white was that?

Rose-Flower

The wind lifting the dust.

Moon-Blossom

     No.   Yes, it was.

Dust from a windflaw blowing down the glen.
There is no rider, Madam.   Shall we sing?

(No answer)

ROSE-FLOWER

She is too stunned with sorrow to give orders.
Shall we not sing, to soothe her?

MOON-BLOSSOM

Sing, then, you.

ROSE-FLOWER

Speak to her first.

MOON-BLOSSOM

Madam——

ROSE-FLOWER

She will not answer;
So speak some quiet thing.

MOON BLOSSOM

Men are like wind-vanes that forever swing;
Men are like winds forever wavering;
Men are like water; men are like the tide;
Women, the rock they ebb from, do abide.

ROSE-FLOWER

She will not speak.   See, it is sunset now,
And now the drums begin upon the housetops
And all the plain spreads out, burningly clear.

JEZEBEL

What is that noise of evil that I hear?

ROSE-FLOWER

The prophet speaking in the market-place.

MOON-BLOSSOM

All afternoon his voice has shouted evil.

JEZEBEL

It is as red as blood within this room.
They have gone out to war; is it not so?
I have been thinking till it all seems plain.
We are amusements only
In mightier life than ours.
God knows, we are not amusement to ourselves.
I am no Queen. I have no son; no husband;
No task, no place, and yet I covet news.
Look, by the rocks, beyond the spur; you see?

ROSE-FLOWER

A rider.

MOON-BLOSSOM

In a white cloak, with a lance.

ROSE-FLOWER

One of King Ahab's lancers, if in white.

MOON-BLOSSOM

Surely a rider from the army, Madam.

ROSE-FLOWER

Bringing good news, because he would not gallop
Save with the news of triumph.

JEZEBEL

What he brings
Will not be what we look for, because life
Is unexpected, whether good or ill.
And at the door by which a horror enters
Another comes, a muffled one, a silent.

(*There is a knocking*)

Enter, without there!

(PHARMAS *enters*)

Yes? What is it, Pharmas?

PHARMAS

The Presence will forgive my interruption.
There is a woman in the outer court
Asks that you grant her audience for a moment.

JEZEBEL

Why should I grant her audience? Who is she?

PHARMAS

She comes from Lower Egypt, as she says.

JEZEBEL

What is her traffic with me?

PHARMAS

Madam, this.

She brings cosmetics and Arabian gums.

JEZEBEL

This is no time for such. I cannot see her.

PHARMAS

May the great Presence pardon if I speak.
I told her that you would not buy her gear
At such a time, but she implored me still
To beg you to admit her to your presence.

JEZEBEL

Did she say why?

PHARMAS

Yes, Madam; because once
Many long years ago she lived in Sidon,
Her father being sutler to the guard,
Your royal father's bodyguardsmen, Madam.
She says she looked upon your presence there,
When you were a princess. She does desire
To see that prophecy of future beauty

Fulfilled in you the Queen, if you the Queen
Would graciously permit her eyes to feast
Upon the sight of you.

JEZEBEL

So our pasts come
To see what time has made of us. So be it.
A word of Sidon would be beauty to me,
To-day. Let her come in.

PHARMAS

I will, O Splendour!

(*Exit*)

ROSE-FLOWER

Queen, is it wise to let a stranger come?

JEZEBEL

No.

MOON-BLOSSOM

Then why see her?

ROSE-FLOWER

Would it not be better
If, first, we questioned her?

MOON-BLOSSOM

Or searched for weapons?

ROSE-FLOWER

She well might carry daggers.

MOON-BLOSSOM

Or bring poison.

JEZEBEL

No; let her come. I am involved in nets
So close, that both the wise thing and unwise
Are cords to catch me.

ROSE-FLOWER

She is here.

PHARMAS (*Entering with* HAMUTAL)

This way.

Stand here until the Presence speaks to you.

(*Exit*)

JEZEBEL

They tell me that you lived in Sidon once.

HAMUTAL

Yes, lady, yes. I passed my childhood there.

JEZEBEL

So. In which street or quarter was your home?

HAMUTAL

The twisted stinking quarter of the poor,
One where you never trod, near the fish-market.

JEZEBEL

I trod there often, and its filthiest lane,
Silvered with cat-gnawn droppings of the nets,
Was blessed to me. It is blest in memory.

HAMUTAL

Perhaps to others it is not so blest.
I know my father starved there; so did I.
That's past. The question now is, Is the man
Gone from the door?

JEZEBEL

The man who brought you here?

Look.

ROSE-FLOWER (*Looking*)

He has gone.

JEZEBEL

Why should he not be gone?

HAMUTAL

They are all spies here, every man of them.
And I have come here, Madam, to say this:
You are in instant danger of your life.

JEZEBEL

From whom?

HAMUTAL

I cannot say. I will not say.
I do not rightly know; but they are wicked;
Wicked and bold. Though others made them so.
I have come here to help you to escape.

JEZEBEL

I thank you for the thought, but first convince me
That there is danger.
I have lived here in danger twenty years.
What horror comes to-day?

HAMUTAL

Come to the window, Madam; but be hidden.
Look there. You see the side gate of the palace?
You see, behind the ruined wall, armed men?
They watch that side gate lest you leave the palace.
Now, on this side, see there, among those bushes
More men-at-arms, watching the royal gate.
There at the water-gate are more armed men,
And they are not your guards.

JEZEBEL

I see they are not.
Then, while they watch for me, their friends are watching
My husband in the army? It is so?

HAMUTAL

No, do not ask me, Madam; I know nothing.

ROSE-FLOWER

How could our Queen escape with the gates watched?
This is some treason, Madam, to betray you
Out of the palace, into savage hands.

JEZEBEL

Let's see her face. Ah! no, she is not that.
Look, woman; many Queens have been betrayed
Since men were ruled; betrayed to death and shame
Most foully, by their subjects, whom they trusted.
There is no treachery on earth more devilish
To brand men blacker or to rake the heart worse.
You would not be the one to tempt me forth
To death and shame among my enemies?

HAMUTAL

Madam, I swear I would not.

MOON-BLOSSOM

We could call

The palace guards.

ROSE-FLOWER

Yes, call the palace guards and question her.

HAMUTAL

Come to the doorway, Madam.
You hear the sounds below? Your palace guards
Are being feasted by your enemies;
Women and drink have overcome your guards.

ROSE-FLOWER

Then how can she escape?

HAMUTAL

The little door—

The little, secret, unsuspected door

Under the stair, leads to a passage way,
Straight to the stables.   I have brought the keys.

JEZEBEL

You are my steward's wife, then?   No one else
Could know about the door.

HAMUTAL

                   Oh, hurry, hurry!
What matter who I am?   You are the Queen.
You will find horses ready in the stables
For you and for your women.   From the stables
You can escape, the postern is unlockt.

JEZEBEL

                          And you?

What kind of life awaits you, after this?

HAMUTAL

A better kind of life than you have made
For poor folk.

JEZEBEL

Ah! fine words; but ten years hence,
Nay, two years, one year, hence, you will remember
My queenship as a dream, a golden dream.

ROSE-FLOWER

O Madam, take the keys; do not delay.

MOON-BLOSSOM

The men outside are beating at the gate.

ROSE-FLOWER

Look, Madam, they have scrambled from the bushes
And beat upon the bars.

HAMUTAL

O Heaven!   Hark!

Jezebel

What is it?

Hamutal

Listen! Listen!

Come from the door.

Rose-Flower

What did you think you heard?

Hamutal

Come nearer me.

Jezebel

I am not terrified.
Draw a deep breath and tell us what it is.

Hamutal

I think that someone is outside the door,
Listening to what we say.

Jezebel

Be still a moment.

Hamutal

It is a man.

Rose-Flower

There is a noise of armour.

Moon-Blossom

Someone is breathing deeply just outside.

Hamutal

What shall I do, what shall I do? O Heaven!

Jezebel

Help her to veil. Treat her as one of you;
Cover her features with the gossamer.
Now let her hurry to the passage yonder.

(*Exit* Hamutal)

We will be ridded of uncertainty.
Is anyone behind the door there? Enter.
  (*She goes back and flings open the door.* PASHUR *is there.*
    He comes in)
Who are you, fellow? And what brings you here?

PASHUR

A messenger, with news. And who are you?

ROSE-FLOWER

She is your Queen, so speak with reverence.

PASHUR

A Queen! God spare us; soldiers own no Queen.
But you shall hear my story, Queen or no.

ROSE-FLOWER

Is the King dead? Speak! Is King Ahab dead?

PASHUR

Learn to respect a royal messenger.
Ay, it has been a hot day's work to-day.

JEZEBEL

If you be from the King, tell us your story.

PASHUR

Ay, I am from the King. That is God's truth.
And I have ridden out, and fought, and ridden
Back to this city, and the whole world sways
As from the falling shoulders of a horse.

ROSE-FLOWER

So the King lives! Thank God.

PASHUR

                Yes, the King lives.
And give God praise, because of victory.

JEZEBEL

I give God praise.

PASHUR

Queen, it has been a day.
Think for a moment what this day has been.
We marched this morning with our banners waving,
With the prophets raving, and the trumpets blowing,
With the charioteers of the King of Judah,
And the spears of the King, a thousand men.
We came to Ramoth when they least expected,
While they slept the noontide and thought it peace.
There we paid back upon the Syrians
A little of what we owed, by God.

JEZEBEL

You mean, they did not know that there was war?

PASHUR

They knew it well enough before we ended.
You see these blackened ashes mixed with blood,
That is what Ramoth and her people are.
The King gave order you should see the work.
You see, ashes and blood; by God, I love them.
But that is not the message that I bring.
I bring a message about good King Ahab,
Who rode into the battle in his chariot
Against the chariots of Syria.
Keep yourself quiet, Syrians, while I tell.
There was a man, who shall be nameless,
Who shall be blameless, or praised aloud,
He with an arrow shot King Ahab
Beneath the arm in the armour joint.

JEZEBEL

He was behind the King, then, when he shot.

PASHUR

He wished his work to be successful, lady.

JEZEBEL

So the King died?

PASHUR

The Queen knows everything.
He did not die at once, but bled to death,
Down in the shadow of the willow trees.
His blood dripped from his chariot; the dogs licked it,
Even as the Teshbon prophet did foretell.

ROSE-FLOWER

Let us mourn for the King, for the cedar fallen,
For the eagle fallen from heaven, for the burnt-out fire.

MOON-BLOSSOM

For the light that shone and is dark, for the word spoken,
For the strength unknit, for the crown brought to the mire.

JEZEBEL

My King is dead! I knew that he was dead.
Have you declared this news to any yet?

PASHUR

Not yet.

JEZEBEL

Then go; declare it to the priests,
That they may now declare it to the people:
The King is dead and now his son is King;
King Joram is the King of Israel.

PASHUR

You are too quick. Joram is not the King.
Jehu, anointed by the Prophet's oil,
Has killed your Joram with an arrow shot
Under his arm, and out right through his heart,

Killing him in his chariot as he drove.
And he has killed his ally, and has flung
Your Joram's body, bloody as it is,
Down into Naboth's vineyard, to the dogs.
Now Bidkar, captain of the charioteers,
Drives the good Jehu hither to be crowned.
Jehu is King, and you, you scarlet whore,
Abominable in the face of God,
You manless, soulless, crownless foreigner,
Shall taste the wrath of God and of God's people.
Now for your spicery there shall be stink,
And where the delicate hair has known the comb
There shall be baldness, and where silk has lain
There shall be nakedness.
And where the red lips mocked God delicately
There shall be broken teeth biting on dust:
It shall be done to you ere this day passes.

(*Exit* PASHUR)

JEZEBEL

My King, my sons, are killed! So Jehu wins.
Thus in an hour the world slips from the feet.
What change beyond this world summons us home?
What conclave of the spirits?

Dead: all three.
Bring me my jewels from the tiring-room.

(*The* MAIDS *go, then return with casket*)

You women, who were with me from the first,
Jehu is coming here to murder me.
He will be here in some few minutes now.
Yet there may still be time for you to go.

ROSE-FLOWER

And time for you, O Queen; you could fly too.

Put on these veils. Oh, hurry! We will take
The door the woman told of, and the horses,
And be in safety on the coast by dawn.

JEZEBEL

I am the daughter of a Queen, my friends.
My life has been here and my death shall be
Near to my dead. But one task more, my friends.
Swift, from within, my cases of cosmetics,
My crownets and the settings for my hair,
The purple chlamys with the spangs of gold
That long ago my father won at Rhodes;
The robe that once the great Queen Helen had
When she was beauty's self, and gave her beauty
To buy a little love in windy Troy.

(*The* MAIDS *bring the gear*)

That is the last task you shall do for me.

(*Gives jewels*)

And this the last least gift that I can give,
With all my thanks for service you have done me,
Year in, year out, for many bitter years.
I think no Queen has ever been so served.
Courage. Here is the key; draw your veils close.

ROSE-FLOWER

O mistress, come with us!

MOON-BLOSSOM
Beloved mistress!
What will they do to us, what will they do?

JEZEBEL

Nothing. They will not find you. You will go
Down through the secret door and so away.
Master your tears. You, take her by the arm.

You will be sailing up the coast to Sidon
By sunrise; think.

MOON-BLOSSOM

And where will you be, lady?

JEZEBEL

As it is written for me.

(*To* ROSE-FLOWER)

Sister. Friend.

When you reach Sidon, greet the King, my father,
And give him this, and bid him consecrate
A stone for me. Now go. The gods go with you.

(*The* MAIDENS *go*)

I will prepare myself for burial,
Since but a little time remains to me.
There is the dust of Jehu's charioting;
The two Assyrian stallions which we gave him
Coming to end my House.

But first, those women.

Hush! All is still. They must have reached the stable.
That woman spoke the truth, the way was clear.
There is no noise of men arresting them.
The guards are still. Thus far they must be safe.
There is no sound; and see, those men are quiet.
O gods, send messengers to make them safe!
Ay, there they go, on horseback. They are free.

Now let me pray. "O thou great fire of life,
Of whom all lives of men are but the sparks,
Take back this spark into the fire that burns
In the great sun, in all the lesser suns,
In the suns' moons, and everything that lives
In wild blood, and the pushing of the spring;
And if my ways were darkness, give me darkness,
And if my ways were brightness, give me light."

Now I will decorate myself for death,
As once before, when I was crowned a bride
Here to the King.
                    First, with this pencil, I
Darken my brows, because they go to death.
And make my eyes bright, since I join my husband
And go again to look upon my sons.
Next I will set this scarlet on my lips,
And on my cheek, lest men should think me pale
And say that I, the Queen, am pale from fear.
Now I will draw Queen Helen's robe about me.
This golden bird is Helen's very hair
That Paris kissed in Troy, my father told me.
Lastly, I will make consecrate my hair
With royal gold, for I will die a Queen.

Now am I as the beauty that I was,
When in my father's palace near the sea
The princes of the Islands came to court me,
Phorbas, and Kreon, and Andemakos,
Kings of the Islands, bright-eyed from the sea,
Men who had gone as strangers to strange lands
And there made friends by something kindling in them:
Not like this Queen whom once they courted there.
Where are they now, those men who loved me once?
Perhaps alive still in their island homes,
Decked with the precious things of half the world,
And thinking of me sometimes, as men do
Think of old loves long over utterly.
And Tsor of Mura, whom I might have married,
Had I been wise.   He will still think of me.
Now will I bare my throat that they may kill me.
How the blood beats that soon will cease to beat,
Poor servant blood, that kept this flesh alive
Knowing not why, and now shall serve no more

This captive soul that was an earthly Queen.
And I without this servant shall not know
The hour of pain, the sleepless night, the day
Anxious as fever with this troublous world;
Shall know, it may be, nothing more forever,
Or know, it may be, all things burningly,
Know god the spirit as a lover would.
Now I will look if those who come to kill
Are on their way.

(Goes to window)

O prison of a city
Which I have hated! Little evil lanes,
Filthy with dogs and lepers and blind men
Made eyeless by the flies. O nest of vipers,
Within few moments I shall pass from you.
Once an Egyptian told me that at death
The soul has power to will its resting-place:
So do I will that I be far from here,
At Sidon on a hilltop near the sea,
Looking at Kittim at a sun-setting,
When all the peaks rise up like crowns of gods
And flame with the gods' thoughts. And past those peaks,
Beyond, in the imagined, never seen,
Behind its reef of rocks, and beautiful
With marble and with wonders and with waters,
Is Mura, where my lover was a King.
But hark, they come. I would go forth to Sidon,
To Sidon, or to Kittim, or to Mura,
Some place of the sea-princes near the sea.
I would forth to Sidon, or to Mura,
To Mura, or to Sidon, or to Kittim—

(She sings)

The april moon is in the sky,
Last night I heard the wild geese cry.
Oh ho!

The brooks are bright on Lebanon,
The rain has come, the snows are gone,
> *Oh ho!*
The north wind faints and soon the south
Will blow the spice smell in the mouth,
> *Oh ho!*
Then shall my bird the ship take wing
And sail the green seas with the King,
And find, maybe, a finer thing
Than any here.
> *Oh ho!*

> (*Enter* PHARMAS *and* ASHOBAL)

PHARMAS

Madam, King Jehu and his men are come:
They ask to see you at the window yonder.

JEHU (*Outside*)

Come out, you Jezebel, and taste God's judgment,
So that this land which you have wrecked may find
Some little peace!

JEZEBEL

> Had Zimri peace,
Who killed his master?

JEHU

Let me see this whore!

> (*He clambers up to look in*)

And who is with her.

> (*Speaks to* PHARMAS *and* ASHOBAL)

Who is on my side?
Who of you men within are for King Jehu?

PHARMAS *and* ASHOBAL

We are, great King!

JEHU

Then throw her down to me,
Seize her and throw her down!

ASHOBAL *and* PHARMAS (*Together*)
(*Throw her down*)

Down with you, Mistress!

JEHU

Get up, you horses. Would you shrink from flesh?
Tread her; come up, you; over her; once more.
Tread her again. I'll teach you who is master.
Ride over her, you fellows, every one.
Ride over her and trample on her body;
Let the beasts kick her. That's the way.
Again.
You tread the harlot who has wrecked this land.
Come here and hold my horses, one of you.
Give me a hand, you men, and let me in.
(*Enter* JEHU *by the window*)
That's made an end of her, the filthy witch!

PHARMAS

I stabbed her with a knife before I threw her.

JEHU

You, did you? Well, then fetch me wine to drink,
In the King's cup, by God, So. Give it here.
(*Drinks*)
I needed drink after this day of fighting.
A hot day's work, but by the living God,
To-morrow shall be hotter. Ahab's sons,
And Ahab's friends, and Ahab's ministers
Shall have their heads in baskets by to-morrow.
Where is this man who says he killed the Queen?

PHARMAS

Here, mighty King.

JEHU

            Go, find the cursed hag
And bury up her carrion in the earth,
For after all she was a King's daughter.

                (Exit PHARMAS)

JEHU *(Sings)*

O out in the desert my bow and my spear,
    Shall win me whatever I need,
Another man's tent, and another man's gear,
    And another man's . . .
Fill me more wine.   Go to the window yonder.
Halt.   As you were.   I'll go myself.   You, fellow.
You fellow, there.   Is the Queen's body there?
What does he say?

ASHOBAL

He says that the wild dogs have torn the body.

JEHU

Good enough end and fitting burial for her!
Now I have sacrifice to do to Baal.
By God, a lusty sacrifice!   By God,
These damned idolaters shall learn the truth!
None of your knives on me.

                (Goes out)

            (The SERVANTS *and* MEN *go out)*

            (Enter MICAIAH *from in front)*

MICAIAH

She was too good a woman to be Queen
In such a land as this, at such a time.
Would she had gone!   Her women have escaped.
And I am freed from prison by the rabble.

Wisdom is gone from the city,
　The killer alone is obeyed,
A man without law, without pity,
　Who was fed by the King he betrayed.
　The debt that was owing is paid,
By a new deed of murder that cries
To the gods who are Kings in the skies.
Though the ways of the gods are most wise,
　They are dark, they make me afraid.

CURTAIN